Religion and Public Life In New England

Falmouth Memorial Library
5 *Lunt Road*
Falmouth, Maine 04105
(207) 781-2351

RELIGION BY REGION

Religion by Region Series
Co-published with the Leonard E. Greenberg Center for the
Study of Religion in Public Life at Trinity College
Mark Silk and Andrew Walsh, Series Editors

The United States is a nation of many distinct regions. But until now, no literature has looked at these regional differences in terms of religion. The Religion by Region Series describes, both quantitatively and qualitatively, the religious character of contemporary America, region by region. Each of the eight regional volumes includes overviews and demographic information to allow comparisons among regions. But at the same time, each volume strives to show what makes its region unique. A concluding volume looks at what these regional variations mean for American religion as a whole.

Religion and Public Life in New England:
Steady Habits, Changing Slowly

Edited by

Andrew Walsh

and

Mark Silk

Published in cooperation with the Leonard E. Greenberg
Center for the Study of Religion in Public Life at
Trinity College, Hartford, Connecticut

ALTAMIRA
PRESS

A Division of
ROWMAN & LITTLEFIELD PUBLISHERS, INC.
Walnut Creek • Lanham • New York • Toronto • Oxford

34105001207312

Published in cooperation with the Leonard E. Greenberg Center for the Study of Religion in Public Life at Trinity College.

ALTAMIRA PRESS
A division of Rowman & Littlefield Publishers, Inc.
1630 North Main Street, #367
Walnut Creek, CA 94596
www.altamirapress.com

Rowman & Littlefield Publishers, Inc.
A wholly owned subsidiary of The Rowman & Littlefield Publishing Group, Inc.
4501 Forbes Boulevard, Suite 200
Lanham, MD 20706

PO Box 317
Oxford
OX2 9RU, UK

Copyright © 2004 by AltaMira Press

All rights reserved. No part of this publication may be reproduced, stored in a retrieval system, or transmitted in any form or by any means, electronic, mechanical, photocopying, recording, or otherwise, without the prior permission of the publisher.

British Library Cataloguing in Publication Information Available

Library of Congress Cataloging-in-Publication Data

Religion and public life in New England : steady habits, changing slowly / edited by Andrew Walsh and Mark Silk.
    p. cm.—(Religion by region ; 3)
    Includes bibliographical references and index.
    ISBN 0-7591-0628-2 (alk. paper)—ISBN 0-7591-0629-0 (pbk. : alk. paper)
    1. New England—Religion. 2. Religion and politics—New England. I. Walsh, Andrew. II. Silk, Mark. III. Title. IV. Series.
    BL2527.N39R45 2004
    200'.974—dc22   2004019135

Printed in the United States of America

♾™ The paper used in this publication meets the minimum requirements of American National Standard for Information Sciences—Permanence of Paper for Printed Library Materials, ANSI/NISO Z39.48–1992.

DEDICATION

For William R. Hutchison
Historian and Teacher

Contents

Preface

Geographical diversity is the hallmark of religion in the United States. There are Catholic zones and evangelical Bible Belts, a Lutheran domain and a Mormon fastness, metropolitan concentrations of Jews and Muslims, and (in a different dimension) parts of the country where religious affiliation of whatever kind is very high and parts where it is far below the norm. This religious heterogeneity is inextricably linked to the character of American places. From Boston to Birmingham, from Salt Lake City to Santa Barbara, even the casual observer perceives public cultures that are intimately connected to the religious identities and habits of the local population.

Yet when the story of religion in American public life gets told, the country's variegated religious landscape tends to be reduced to a series of monochrome portraits of the spiritual state of the union, of piety along the Potomac, of great events or swings of mood that raise or lower the collective religious temperature. Whatever the virtues of compiling such a unified national narrative—and I believe they are considerable—it obscures a great deal. As the famous red-and-blue map of the 2000 presidential vote makes clear, region has not ceased to matter in national politics. Indeed, in this era of increasing federalism, regions are, state by state, charting ever more distinctive courses.

To understand where each region is headed and why, it is critical to recognize the place of religion in it.

Religion by Region, a project of the Leonard E. Greenberg Center for the Study of Religion in Public Life at Trinity College in Hartford, represents the first comprehensive effort to show how religion shapes, and is being shaped by, regional culture in America. The project has been designed to produce edited volumes (of which this is the third) on each of eight regions of the country. A ninth volume will sum up the results in order to draw larger conclusions about the way religion and region combine to affect civic culture and public policy in the United States as a whole.

The purpose of the project is not to decompose a national storyline into eight separate narratives. Rather, it is to bring regional realities to bear, in a systemat-

7

ic way, on how American culture is understood at the beginning of the twenty-first century. In line with the Greenberg Center's commitment to enhance public understanding of religion, these volumes are intended for a general audience, with a particular eye towards helping working journalists make better sense of the part religion plays in the public life—local, statewide, regional, and national—that they cover. At the same time, I am persuaded that the accounts and analyses provided in these volumes will make a significant contribution to the academic study of religion in contemporary America.

The project's division of the country into regions will be generally familiar, with the exception of what we are calling the Southern Crossroads—a region roughly equivalent to what American historians know as the Old Southwest, comprising Louisiana, Texas, Arkansas, Oklahoma, and Missouri. Since we are committed to covering every state in the Union (though not the territories—e.g., Puerto Rico), Hawaii has been included in a Pacific region with California and Nevada, and Alaska in the Pacific Northwest.

Cultural geographers may be surprised to discover a few states out of their customary places. Idaho, which is usually considered part of the Pacific Northwest, has been assigned to the Mountain West. In our view, the fact that the bulk of Idaho's population lives in the heavily Mormon southern part of the state links it more closely to Utah than to Oregon and Washington. To be sure, we might have chosen to parcel out certain states between regions, assigning northern Idaho and western Montana to the Pacific Northwest or, to take another example, creating a Catholic band running from southern Louisiana through south Texas and across the lower tiers of New Mexico and Arizona on into southern California. The purpose of the project, however, is not to map the country religiously but to explore the ways that politics, public policies, and civil society relate—or fail to relate—to the religion that is on the ground. States have had to be kept intact because when American laws are not made in Washington, D.C. they are made in statehouses. To understand what is decided in Baton Rouge, Louisiana's Catholic south and evangelical north must be seen as engaged in a single undertaking.

That is not to say that the details of American religious demography are unimportant to our purpose. That demography has undergone notable shifts in recent years, and these have affected public life in any number of ways. To reckon with them, it has been essential to assemble the best data available on the religious identities of Americans and how they correlate with voting patterns and views on public issues. As students of American religion know, however, this is far from an easy task. The U.S. Census is prohibited by law from asking questions about religion, and membership reports provided by religious bodies to nongovernmental researchers—when they are provided at all—vary greatly in accuracy. Most public opinion polling does not enable us to draw precise correlations between respondents' views on issues and their religious identity and behavior.

In order to secure the best possible empirical grounding, the project has assembled a range of data from three sources, which are described in detail in the Appendix. These have supplied us with, among other things, information from religious bodies on their membership; from individuals on their religious identities; and from voters in specific religious categories on their political preferences and opinions. (For purposes of clarity, people are described as "adherents" or "members" only when reported as such by a religious institution. Otherwise, they are "identifiers.") Putting this information together with 2000 census and other survey data, the project has been able to create both the best available picture of religion in America today and the most comprehensive account of its political significance.

Religion by Region does not argue that religion plays the same kind of role in each region of the country; nor does it mean to advance the proposition that religion is the master key that unlocks all the secrets of American public life. As the tables of contents of the individual volumes make clear, each region has its distinctive religious layout, based not only on the numerical strength of particular religious bodies but also on how those bodies, or groups of them, function on the public stage. In some regions, religion serves as a shaping force; in others it is a subtler conditioning agent. Our objective is simply to show what the picture looks like from place to place and to provide consistent data and a framework of discussion sufficient to enable useful contrasts and comparisons to be drawn.

A project of such scope and ambition does not come cheap. We are deeply indebted to the Lilly Endowment for making it possible.

Mark Silk
Hartford, Connecticut
May 2004

Introduction

Religion in New England: Reckoning with Catholicism

Andrew Walsh

In a recently published historical atlas of religion in America, Bret E. Carroll notes that many informed observers think "mass culture, mass media, and interregional migration have operated to homogenize American life and erase regional religious differences."[1] We, on the contrary, begin with the observation that any such creeping homogenization is barely discernable in New England. No one entertains the slightest doubt about where New England is, or what it is like. It may be hard to imagine someone saying, "That's a real Mid-Atlantic thing to do." And one may legitimately wonder about how to deal with places like Louisiana, Idaho, Florida, or Missouri, which are so clearly divided into two or more cultural zones. But contemporary residents of New England embrace with zest the regional identity that history has bestowed on them. They routinely call themselves New Englanders and baptize all sorts of things as distinctively characteristic of the region, from voting patterns to accents to weather to bad driving.

When, in 1961, the geographer Wilber Zelinsky divided the United States into seven major and four minor regions, New England was the only part of the country where the boundaries of a "religious region" coincided exactly with state borders.[2] Maine, New Hampshire, Vermont, Massachusetts, Rhode Island, and Connecticut—the six New England states—share a lively, persistent, deep-rooted, and coherent regional identity, one in which the religious balance of forces plays a lively, constitutive, but not always obvious role in public life. Three salient religious characteristics shape New England's distinctive regional identity.

At the top of the list is the overwhelming Roman Catholic presence in the region. According to the North American Religion Atlas (NARA), almost 70 percent of the New Englanders who claim a religious identity are Catholics. And in many parts of the region, especially in urbanized southern New England, Catholics make up the outright majority of the population. New England is, by a comfortable margin, the most intensely Catholic region in the United States. Indeed, cities like Providence, Rhode Island, Springfield, Massachusetts, and Waterbury, Connecticut, are just about as Catholic as Salt Lake City is Mormon. Further, New England's Catholic population is more homogeneous than that of other American regions. Descendents of immigrants from Ireland still dominate the region's Catholic population, although there are many descendents of immigrants from French Canada and Italy.

Second, mainline Protestantism remains a significant force in New England, a region where moderate and liberal mainline Protestants outnumber conservative Protestants by at least two to one (the reverse of the ratio that prevails in the nation at large). Beyond the question of their numbers, mainline Protestants are active custodians of New England's intensely local civic culture, which is focused on the town, an institution accorded virtually sacred status. The mainline churches—so frequently symbolic presences on the town green—nourish a sense of connection to the region's distinctive colonial past, when Congregationalism was the established state religion in many parts of the region for almost two centuries and was influential even in states like Rhode Island and Vermont where it was never legally established.

Finally, the region's life still bears the marks of the long struggle between Protestants and Catholics that began in the 1840s, when massive immigration by Catholics from Ireland began. Within a few decades, Catholics outnumbered Protestants in New England. But the deep-rooted cultural and economic advantages enjoyed by the Yankees made them formidable combatants. They gave ground grudgingly, using a wide range of tools to maintain their ascendancy, beginning with economic and political power but eventually incorporating the public schools, public libraries, and museums among other social service and cultural organizations, to hem in Catholic communal power. Catholics responded with aggressive self-assertion, but—fatefully—they preferred to build a self-sufficient, semi-detached subculture anchored in the region's industrial towns and cities. Although, over time, Catholics "took over" many Yankee institutions—the public school systems most notably—the lag was often very lengthy. In the meantime, New England developed a dual institutional culture, where separate and contending "Catholic" and "Protestant" schools, colleges, hospitals, orphanages, cemeteries, and even professional and cultural associations came to seem perfectly natural.

This vigorous rivalry persisted for more than a century and was resolved, in the decades after World War II, not with outright victory, but with a kind of unspoken truce—a truce in which those on both sides still take some care not to upset the delicate balance of forces. In this mood, religion is treated as a force with great divisive potential. In New England, it is therefore often addressed obliquely or not at all.

This nuance of New England's regional culture is not widely appreciated outside the region. One of the first major signs of trouble in one-time front-runner Howard Dean's campaign for the Democratic Party's 2004 presidential nomination arose from his difficulties with public discussion of religious faith—something all American presidential aspirants must handle competently. "I'm still learning a lot about faith and the South and how important it is," Dean, the former governor of Vermont, ineptly remarked in January of 2004, just a few days before the Iowa caucuses. Widely criticized—perhaps mocked is a better term—for his fumbling attempts to characterize his quite possibly non-existent religious beliefs, Dean later told a group of reporters traveling with him on a campaign plane, "I'm a New Englander, so I'm not used to wearing religion on my sleeve and being open about it." Dean's explanation didn't persuade many people on the national stage, but in the context of New England it made some sense. The region's politicians have little to gain by triggering the polarizing animosities that sometimes, on some issues, lie close to the surface.

Nevertheless, it would be ludicrous to portray New England life as an unending, unchanging wrestling match between Catholics and mainline Protestants. The Jewish and African-American Protestant communities, roughly comparable in size, have been energetic and well organized actors in New England for decades. Newer forces for change are also making themselves felt at several levels. On the one hand, new populations are moving into the region, including people of color, although they are doing so more slowly than in many other parts of the nation. Conservative Protestants, once virtually invisible, are, although still few in number, now easily visible in New England. Muslims, Hindus, Buddhists, Sikhs, and other practitioners of non-Western religions are present in many parts of the region, in still smaller numbers. And these groups are beginning to make themselves felt in the region's public life.

It is also important to add that many of New England's residents don't connect themselves with religion. Indeed, many Americans think of New England as a hotbed of secularity—probably more so than is actually the case. NARA, which tracks the number of adherents claimed by religious groups, reports that 38.5 percent of New Englanders are unaffiliated or uncounted, just below the national average of 40.6 percent. Undercutting that rather substantial figure, the 2001 American Religion Identity Survey (ARIS), which reports the responses of individuals to a random telephone survey, indicates that 21.7 percent of New England's adults say they have no religion or are humanists, a bit higher than the national average of 19.6 percent. So, in New England as in other parts of the nation, a very substantial number of people who do not belong to religious organizations nevertheless *think* of themselves as religious, and, indeed, as members of a particular religious group.

Overall, the most dramatic changes that have taken place in recent decades have worked *within* the major blocks of New England's population. The biggest shift since the mid-twentieth century has been the movement of the Catholic population up the socioeconomic ladder and out of cities to the suburbs. Prosperous suburban Catholics, who now make up New England's Catholic core constituency, mix easily with middle-class Protestants and secular citizens, and often vote like them.

If Catholic voters were ever "priest-ridden" (the abiding bogey-man of centuries worth of New England Protestants), they certainly aren't now. For example, New England's Catholic voters often take public policy positions at odds with official Catholic teaching. Exit polling surveys on political opinions from the last three presidential elections show that the positions that white, Catholic New Englanders take on abortion are far more likely to be pro-choice (45.7 percent) or moderate (18.9 percent) than pro-life (35.4 percent). And whether they are Democrats or Republicans, Catholic politicians in New England—a very large group—very rarely try to make their way as pro-life standard bearers. Contemporary New England Catholics are also more likely to be registered as independents than New England Catholics of the early and middle twentieth century, who were overwhelmingly Democrats and often very closely tied to trade unions.

While both Catholic and mainline Protestant identities are still strongly held, many Catholics and Protestants are more loosely tied to their institutions than was once the case. American Catholics remain less likely than practitioners of most other religions to switch their religious commitment, but the intensity of Catholic participation has fallen quite dramatically since the 1960s. According to surveys, the number of Catholics who attend Mass at least once a week ranges between 30 and 40 percent—quite a bit lower than the levels that prevailed as recently as the 1970s. And it is the political views of "low-commitment" Catholics (those who attend religious services less than once a week), mainline Protestants, and evangelicals that lie closest to the regional averages for all voters in presidential exit polling surveys. The $64,000 question, for those seeking to understand the contemporary state of religious influence in public life, may well be: Why is there so little difference between the voting patterns of New England Catholics and secular New Englanders?

Finally, as this is written in the spring of 2004, New England's religious state of mind remains unsettled by the impact of the Catholic clerical sexual abuse scandal that shook the region like an earthquake in the months after January 2002. Boston and eastern New England have been the epicenter of that scandal, and the immense outrage that has gripped the region serves as strong but indirect evidence of Catholicism's continuing centrality in New England life.

It is the mission of the authors of this volume to explore these dynamics and to explain how they are shaping the contemporary role of religion in New England public life. We have chosen to approach the subject by focusing on religious traditions as the main framework for discussion. Other approaches—state-by-state analysis or organization by theme such as civic religious traditions or immigrant approaches—might also be illuminating. But given the strength and salience of denominational identity in New England, and especially of Roman Catholic identity, it seemed best to focus on religious tradition. The chapters that follow will not provide exhaustive analyses of everything worth knowing about the religious traditions involved. That's not only impossible given the scope of this book, but unwise, since that would inevitably blur the focus on the central question at hand: how religion shapes and is shaped by the region's public life.

Like every volume of the Religion by Region series, this book opens with an overview of the religious demography of the region, in this case a chapter called "The Demographic Layout: A Tale of Two New Englands." Stephen Prothero, associate professor of religion and chairman of the religion department at Boston University, begins with a summary of the demographic factors that make the region distinctive, mostly with data drawn from the 2000 United States Census. He then reports on the current religious demography of the region, and offers a brief historical account of the complex relationship among Protestants, Catholics, and others. Prothero draws attention to the existence of "two New Englands." The first is the lightly populated northern tier of states—Vermont, New Hampshire, and Maine, which have changed a great deal in recent decades, an area where religion is notably weaker as a public force. The second comprises the densely populated states of southern New England, the heartland of contemporary New England. Keenly interested in the movement of Asian religious traditions into the United States, Prothero also reports on the growing presence of Islam, Hinduism, Buddhism, and other Asian religions, as well as in the growing importance of immigration.

The immense role of Catholicism is addressed in two chapters. James O'Toole, professor of history at Boston College, offers a historical introduction that focuses on Catholic approaches to public life as they unfolded over the past 150 years. His "Majority Faith with a Minority Mindset" also addresses the political culture of New England Catholics. "In the Flux of Crisis," by Michele Dillon, associate professor of sociology at the University of New Hampshire, explores the impact of institutional Catholicism in the region. She deals with the structure of Catholic life—the parish, the diocese, and other Catholic organizations—and also with the varying ways in which contemporary Catholics define their relationship to the institutional Church. Both authors address the current clerical sexual abuse scandal, but Dillon's chapter includes an extended discussion of the crisis' impact on Catholic attitudes and behaviors.

Chapter Three, with two major sections, then deals with the role of Protestants. In the first section, called "Mainline Protestants: Custodians of Community," Maria E. Erling, associate professor of the history of Christianity in North America and global mission at the Lutheran Theological Seminary at Gettysburg, and a former Lutheran pastor and denominational official in New England, offers an analysis of the ways mainline Protestants are struggling to retain their historic influence in the region. Her treatment emphasizes the powerful civic focus of mainline Protestantism and analyzes the ways in which Protestants have approached participation in public life in recent decades, often through the instrument of ecumenical and interfaith organizations. The second section, called "Conservative Protestants: Prospering on the Margins" treats the revival of conservative Protestantism in the region since the 1960s. This sub- chapter, written by Andrew Walsh, explores the growth of evangelicalism, fundamentalism, and Pentecostalism, first around military installations, then in the region's new suburbs, and currently among immigrants, particularly Latinos and Asians.

A final chapter, by Daniel Terris, director of the International Center for Ethics, Justice, and Public Life at Brandeis University, explores the ways in which Jews and African-American Protestants have approached public life in the region. Both religious communities are of long standing in New England, and both have been extremely well organized participants in public dialogues, especially since the 1950s. While significant, both communities are rather small and concentrated in a handful of metropolitan areas. Both religious communities have consistently sought "a place at the table," and have designed many of their public strategies in response to the civic public stances and organizational approaches of mainline Protestants. While different in many important ways, both New England's Jewish and African-American Protestant communities face the challenges that grow out of the diffusion of group members into New England's suburbs.

The book concludes with a discussion of how the pieces fit together, written by Andrew Walsh. Its general thesis is reflected in the subtitle of this book: "Steady Habits, Changing Slowly."

It is also fair to alert readers that, as graduate students at Harvard University during the 1980s, four of the authors began a discussion of the role of religion in American public life. Maria Erling, Stephen Prothero, Daniel Terris and Andrew Walsh studied together with William R. Hutchison, Charles Warren Research Professor of the History of Religion in America at Harvard Divinity School. We all participated in his project exploring the history of the Protestant establishment in America. All of us are proud to name Bill as our teacher. This volume is dedicated to him.

Endnotes

1. Brett E. Carroll, *The Routledge Historical Atlas of Religion in America* (New York: Routledge, 2000): 131.

2. Wilber Zelinsky, "An Approach to the Religious Geography of the United States: Patterns of Church Membership in 1952," *Annals of the Association of American Geographers* 51 (June 1961): 139-193.

RELIGIOUS AFFILIATION IN NEW ENGLAND AND THE NATION

The charts on the following pages compare two measures of religious identification: self-identification by individuals responding to a survey and adherents claimed by religious institutions. The charts compare regional data for New England and national data for both measures. The sources of the data are described below.

On page 20
Adherents Claimed by Religious Groups

The Polis Center at Indiana University-Purdue University Indianapolis provided the Religion by Region Project with estimates of adherents claimed by religious groups in New England and the nation at large. These results are identified as the North American Religion Atlas (NARA). NARA combines 2000 Census data with the Glenmary Research Center's 2000 Religious Congregations and Membership Survey (RCMS). Polis Center demographers supplemented the RCMS reports with data from other sources to produce estimates for groups that did not report to Glenmary.

On page 21
Religious Self-Identification

Drawn from the American Religious Identification Survey (ARIS 2001), these charts contrast how Americans in New England and the nation at large describe their own religious identities. The ARIS study, conducted by Barry A. Kosmin, Egon Mayer, and Ariela Keysar at the Graduate Center of the City University of New York, includes the responses of 50,283 U.S. households gathered in a series of national, random-digit dialing, telephone surveys.

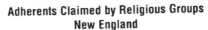

Adherents Claimed by Religious Groups
New England

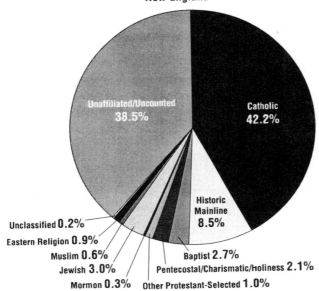

Unaffiliated/Uncounted
38.5%

Catholic
42.2%

Historic
Mainline
8.5%

Unclassified 0.2%
Eastern Religion 0.9%
Muslim 0.6%
Jewish 3.0%
Mormon 0.3%

Baptist 2.7%
Pentecostal/Charismatic/Holiness 2.1%
Other Protestant-Selected 1.0%

Adherents Claimed by Religious Groups
National

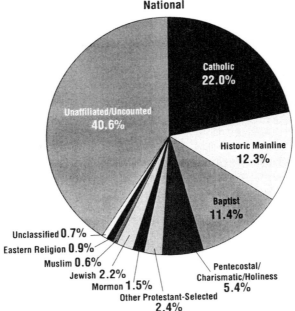

Unaffiliated/Uncounted
40.6%

Catholic
22.0%

Historic Mainline
12.3%

Baptist
11.4%

Unclassified 0.7%
Eastern Religion 0.9%
Muslim 0.6%
Jewish 2.2%
Mormon 1.5%
Other Protestant-Selected
2.4%

Pentecostal/
Charismatic/Holiness
5.4%

Religious Self-Identification
New England

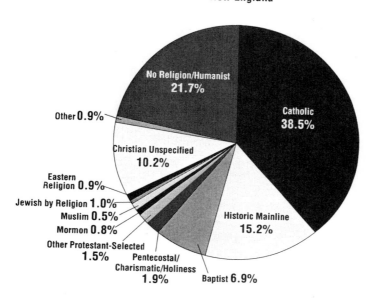

Religious Self-Identification
National

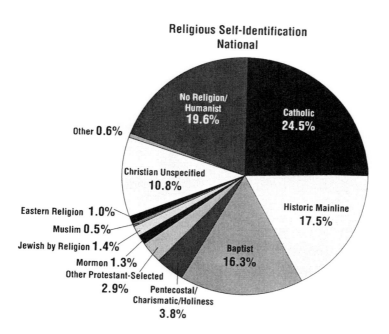

CHAPTER ONE

THE DEMOGRAPHIC LAYOUT: A TALE OF TWO NEW ENGLANDS

Stephen Prothero

With only 5 percent of the U.S. population and 2 percent of its land mass, New England is the country's smallest region geographically and its second smallest in population. Nonetheless, New Englanders share a strong sense of regional identity, rooted in shared memories of colonial history, liberal political commitments, a town-based civic culture, and a connection to the sea. Religiously, New England has pressed far beyond its roots as a Congregationalist stronghold. Like the rest of the country, it is now quite diverse in religious terms, with Sikh gurdwaras, Islamic mosques, and Jain temples punctuating its skylines. Still it remains a distinct religious region by virtue of its staunch Catholicism: New England today is nearly as Catholic as Utah is Mormon.

According to the 2000 U.S. Census, the total population of the six New England states is 13.9 million. The most populous is the Commonwealth of Massachusetts, with 6.3 million people, followed by Connecticut (3.4 million), Maine (1.3 million), New Hampshire (1.2 million), Rhode Island (1.0 million), and Vermont (600,000). While New England's population rose 5 percent between 1990 and 2000 (almost all of that due to immigration), the overall U.S. population rose at a much faster 13 percent clip.

New England's literary lights—and there have been many—have typically sung the praises of rural New England. But most of the region's inhabitants are clustered around three metropolitan corridors: from Providence north through Boston and Worcester into southern New Hampshire; from Springfield to Hartford; and from New Haven westward along Long Island Sound, the area that makes up Connecticut's contribution to the tri-state New York metropolitan region. Many of New England's 67 counties, however, are overwhelmingly rural, and rural folks outnumber urban dwellers in both Vermont and Maine. Maine has a population density of only 41 per square mile, and Vermont of just 66. Massachusetts, by contrast, squeezes over 800 people into each square mile of its territory, and Rhode Island in excess of 1,000. Given these disparities, it makes sense to conceive of New England in terms of two distinct sub-regions: a rural north and an urban south. This can be seen in Figure 1.1

New England has a reputation for being lily white, and that reputation is largely deserved, especially in the rural north. African Americans constitute less than 1 percent of all residents of Maine, New Hampshire, and Vermont, and at least 96 percent of the population in each of those states is white. But the picture in the urban south is quite different. African Americans are a sizeable minority in Connecticut (9 percent of the population), Massachusetts (5 percent), and Rhode Island (4 percent). And 93 percent of the immigrants who arrived in New England between 1990 and 2000 came to one of those three states.

Like African Americans, Latinos are strikingly underrepresented in New England. Only 30 percent of foreign-born New Englanders hail from Latin America (the lowest figure of any region in the country), and Spanish is spoken in just 6 percent of all households. Still, Latinos comprise 9 percent of the population in Connecticut and Rhode Island, and 7 percent in Massachusetts. But those figures are rising rapidly. Between 1990 and 2000, the Latino population in New England jumped 54 percent to 875,225, more than the entire population of Vermont.

Not surprisingly, Canadian Americans are over-represented in New England; 7 percent of all foreign-born New Englanders hail from Canada—the highest regional figure in the 2000 Census, and well above the national average of 3 percent. New England also has the highest percentage (13 percent) of households in which a language other than English or Spanish is spoken. That distinction is attributable to the many French speakers in the region's northern reaches, and to recent immigrants from Asia in the urban south. Although New England cannot match the Pacific Northwest when it comes to Asian immigration, a fairly high percentage (23 percent) of its foreign-born population was born in Asia. In fact, there are more Asian Americans than African Americans in Maine, New Hampshire, and Vermont.

Asian Americans have a particularly strong presence in Lowell, Massachusetts, which has become a Mecca of sorts for South Asian immigrants in the United States. Thanks to a major influx of Southeast Asians, the Asian American population in Lowell swelled 50 percent between 1990 and 2000, and people of Asian ancestry now constitute 17 percent of that city's population. In fact, Lowell now boasts the second largest Cambodian population in the United States (behind only Long Beach, California) and one of the most intriguing complexes of Cambodian, Laotian, and Vietnamese Buddhist temples.

Figure 1.1   Map of New England Population

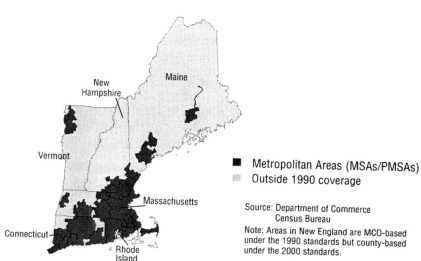

■ Metropolitan Areas (MSAs/PMSAs)
▨ Outside 1990 coverage

Source: Department of Commerce
Census Bureau

Note: Areas in New England are MCO-based
under the 1990 standards but county-based
under the 2000 standards.

Another New England city undergoing rapid diversification is Lewiston, Maine. Here the arrival of Somalis, most of them Muslims, has quickly transformed a stronghold of French-Canadian Catholicism into a multi-ethnic and multi-religious city. According to some estimates, well over 1,000 arrived over the last few years of the twentieth century and the first few years of the twenty-first century—a significant influx for a blue-collar town of approximately 36,000. There is also a sizeable Somali community in Portland, Maine. Thanks to migrations such as these, New England has a larger portion of Africans (5 percent) in its foreign-born population than any other region in the county.

New England is home to roughly 260 colleges and universities and its people are highly educated. Thirty-one percent of its adults 25 years and older hold a bachelor's degree—the country's highest rate of higher education, and well above the national average of 24 percent. This percentage varies considerably, however, from state to state: from a high of 33 percent in Massachusetts to a low of 23 percent in Maine.

Given these education levels, it should not be surprising that New England is the most white-collar region in the country. With over 6,000 miles of coastline stretching alongside five of its states—only Vermont is landlocked—New England traditionally based its economy on the ocean, especially whaling and fishing, and later on tourism as well. Today, however, 38.5 percent of its employed adults work in management and professional occupations, considerably above the national average of 34 percent.

Such jobs provide New Englanders with excellent incomes. According to the 2000 Census, per-capita income was $21,587 for the nation as a whole. Two New England states, Maine and Vermont, came in under that figure at $19,533 and $20,625, respectively. But the other four states came in higher, with Connecticut ($28,766) and Massachusetts ($25,952) ranking first and third in the nation. Only 9 percent of the New England population—the lowest figure of any region in the nation—lives in poverty.

Throughout its history, New England has given birth to liberal theologians and denominations. Massachusetts was a haven for Unitarianism and the birthplace of Transcendentalism, and today that state has more members of the Unitarian Universalist Association than any other. New Englanders lean to the left when it comes to politics too. All the New England states, with the notable exception of New Hampshire, voted for Al Gore in the 2000 presidential election. And there may be no more liberal state than Vermont. Its sole representative in the House of Representatives, Independent Bernie Sanders, is a socialist.

Like Sanders, New Englanders like to think of themselves as Independents rather than party partisans. According to the American Religious Identification Survey (ARIS) conducted in 2001, 41 percent of New Englanders call themselves Independents, with 27 percent preferring the Democrats and 25 percent the Republicans. Moreover, Protestants and Catholics in the region are both far more likely to call themselves Independents than their counterparts in the nation as a whole. Still, New England residents across the religious spectrum show a decided preference for liberal political causes. A series of polls conducted by the Bliss Center at the University of Akron in 1992, 1996, and 2000 identified New England as the region most committed to environmental protection, national health insurance, gay rights, abortion rights, and helping minorities. When asked to describe their position on homosexuality, for example, 67 percent of New Englanders said they favored gay rights, well above the national rate of 57 percent.

Catholics and "Nones"

Students of colonial history—at least the sort of colonial history that begins in 1620 with the Pilgrims in Plymouth—will remember New England as a Puritan-dominated Congregationalist stronghold. In fact, while most states gave up government-sponsored religion following the ratification of the First Amendment to the U.S. Constitution in 1791, Congregational establishment endured as late as 1818 in Connecticut and 1833 in Massachusetts. Today, Congregational churches still stand at the center of many New England towns, but Roman Catholicism has long been the dominant religious force in the region.

The two main data sets informing this volume—the ARIS and the North American Religion Atlas (NARA)—measure different things (ARIS measures

Figure 1.2   Catholics, Residents, and Adherence Rate for 2000 (NARA)

	Catholics	Residents	Adherence Rate
Rhode Island	542,244	1,048,319	0.517251
Massachusetts	3,092,296	6,349,097	0.487045
Connecticut	1,372,562	3,405,565	0.403035
New Hampshire	431,259	1,235,786	0.348975
Vermont	147,918	608,827	0.242956
Maine	283,024	1,274,923	0.221993
New England	5,869,303	13,922,517	0.421569

self-identification and NARA measures group affiliation, as reported by denominational rolls) so they come up with different numbers for New England's Catholics. Yet each recognizes New England as the nation's Catholic region par excellence. Thirty-eight percent of the New Englanders interviewed by ARIS telephone researchers self-identify as Catholics. According to NARA researchers, who compiled data on 149 religious bodies, 42 percent of the region's residents are affiliated with the Catholic Church.

The NARA survey identified Rhode Island and Massachusetts as the most Catholic states in the nation, with adherence rates of 52 percent and 49 percent, respectively, in 2000. Connecticut (40 percent) and New Hampshire (35 percent) are in the top 10, and Vermont (24 percent) and Maine (22 percent) in the top 20. According to the NARA data, Rhode Island's capital city, Providence, is the most Catholic city in the nation, with 53 Catholics per 100 residents; the Boston metropolitan area (49 percent) is nipping at its heels. This is seen in Figure 1.2.

The ARIS numbers come in a bit different, but Catholic dominance is clear here as well. According to ARIS's researchers, 38 percent of New Englanders identify themselves as Catholic: 51 percent in Rhode Island, 44 percent in Massachusetts, 38 percent in Vermont, 35 percent in New Hampshire, 32 percent in Connecticut, and 24 percent in Maine.

Although the rural north is not as inclined to Catholicism as is the urban south, Catholics dominate in the far reaches of the region, where French-Canadian influence seeps over the border. Aroostook County, the largest and northernmost in the region, is according to NARA also the most Catholic county in Maine, with a ratio of Catholics to residents of 43 percent. Catholicism is more dominant in New Hampshire's Coos County and Vermont's Grand Isle County (both touching the Canadian border) where Catholics constitute 54 percent and 57 percent of residents, respectively. Catholics also outnumber all other residents in most counties in Rhode Island and Massachusetts.

In the halls of power, Catholicism predominates as well. At the turn of the twenty-first century, both of Massachusetts' U.S. senators were Catholics, as were six of its 10 U.S. representatives and its governor. At the state level, Catholic politicians were even more entrenched, accounting for 75 percent of both the Massachusetts State Senate and House of Representatives.

Although New England remains the nation's Catholic hothouse, there are some indications that Catholic dominance is slipping. Between 1990 and 2000, the U.S. Catholic population rose 16 percent, according to NARA , and its growth was even more spectacular in the West (42 percent) and the South (30 percent), which benefited from large influxes of Spanish-speaking Catholics. Over that same decade, the Catholic population also grew in Massachusetts, Maine, Vermont, and New Hampshire. Still, with the notable exception of New Hampshire, where the number of Catholics rose 45 percent, that expansion was modest at best—well below the national level—in part because Latin American immigration to the region was so meager. In Rhode Island and Connecticut, the number of Catholic residents actually declined. In all the New England states except Rhode Island, the total number of Catholic congregations fell too. While there is still a Catholic congregation in every county in New England, only 20 percent of all the congregations in the region are Catholic churches.

Between 1990 and 2000, Rhode Island, Massachusetts, and Connecticut all saw declines in their ratios of Catholics to residents. The NARA data reveal a particularly severe dip in Rhode Island: from 63 percent of its population to 52 percent in just 10 years. In fact, Rhode Island posted the largest loss of Catholics, in percentage terms, of any state in the country between 1990 and 2000.

Mainline Protestants have a presence in New England, though they by no means dominate as they once did. Nearly one out of every four United Church of Christ (U.C.C.) members, and one out of every seven Episcopalians, live in New England, yet the U.C.C. accounts for only 2.4 percent of all New Englanders and the Episcopalians for only 1.7 percent.

Mainline Protestant denominations are all over-represented when it comes to the region's religious landscape, where the ghosts of the mainline's past dominance linger in plain view. In most New England towns, "First Church" is Congregational. In fact, 13 percent of all congregations in New England are affiliated with the U.C.C. and another 7.4 percent with the Episcopalians. United Methodists (8.4 percent of all congregations and 1.4 percent of adherents) also have much higher visibility in New England cities and towns than their raw numbers would justify. While Catholics pack 3,206 adherents into each of their parishes, the average United Methodist church serves only 243.

Evangelical Protestant denominations are even weaker than their mainline counterparts. In fact, Rhode Island is the least evangelical state in the country

Figure 1.3   Denominational "Winners" and "Losers" in Massachusetts, 1990-2000

	Percentage Gain/Loss
Church of the Nazarene	51.9%
Latter-day Saints	47.8%
Assemblies of God	23.0%
Southern Baptists	8.9%
Overall Population	**5.4%**
Catholics	4.4%
Lutherans (ELCA)	0.3%
Jews	-3.1%
United Church of Christ	-10.4%
United Methodists	-10.9%
Episcopalians	-19.0%
American Baptists	-20.3%
Unitarian-Universalists	-27.8%

and, in a ranking of all 50 states by adherence rates in evangelical denominations, all six New England states sit in the bottom 10. Pentecostal/Charismatic/ Holiness traditions are far less potent in New England than they are in the rest of the nation, and the born-again megachurches that have taken other regions by storm have not yet gained traction in these seaside states. Baptists, for example, are notably quiescent; while 16.3 percent of all Americans told ARIS researchers they were Baptists, only 6.9 percent of New Englanders did. In New England as a whole, the ratio of mainline Protestants to evangelical Protestants is nearly 3:1.

Yet the evangelicals are coming on. In Massachusetts, mainline denominations such as the Episcopal Church, the American Baptist Churches in the USA, the United Methodist Church, and the United Church of Christ all lost members between 1990 and 2000. And while the Evangelical Lutheran Churches of America (E.L.C.A.) made nominal gains, it failed to keep up with the expansion of the population. Pentecostal and evangelical groups, by contrast, posted strong gains, with the Assemblies of God up 23 percent and the Church of the Nazarene expanding 52 percent. The Latter-day Saints, which dedicated a new temple in Belmont, Massachusetts, in 2000, grew 48 percent. Even the Southern Baptist Convention, a real fish out of water in the New England region, expanded 9 percent. This can be seen in Figure 1.3.

Figures 1.4 and 1.5 show the NARA data for adherents to various religions in New England (1.4) and, in comparison, in the United States (1.5).

In New Hampshire, the story is strikingly similar. Although this state saw its

Figure 1.4 Number of Adherents in New England by Religious Family (NARA)			
Religious Family, Rank Ordered	Percent of Adherents	Percent of Total Population	Percent of All Adherents
1. Catholic	5,869,303	42.2	68.5
2. Jewish	417,675	3.0	4.8
3. Historically African-Amer. Protestant	356,666	2.6	4.2
4. UCC	340,476	2.4	4.0
5. Episcopalians	240,374	1.7	2.8
6. Baptist	231,295	1.6	2.7
7. United Methodist	193,419	1.4	2.3
8. Other Conservative Christian	165,458	1.2	1.9
9. Holiness/Wesleyan/Pentecostal	154,639	1.1	1.8
10. Asian Religions	129,733	0.9	1.5
11. Orthodox Christian	125,764	0.9	1.5
12. Muslim	77,662	0.6	0.9
13. Lutheran (ELCA)	76,145	0.5	0.9
14. Confessional/Reformed Non-UCC Cong.	71,330	0.5	0.8
15. Other Mainline Prot/Liberal Christian	47,330	0.3	0.6
16. LDS (Mormon)	44,803	0.3	0.5
17. Presbyterian U.S.A.	21,100	0.2	0.2
18. Pietist/Anabaptist	1,792	0.0	0.0
19. Christians (Disciples)	900	0.0	0.0
Total	8,566,483	61.5	100.0
Unaffiliated	5,356,034	38.5	N/A

overall population swell 11 percent between 1990 and 2000, the American Baptists, Episcopalians, the United Methodists, and the United Church of Christ all lost adherents, while groups such as the Salvation Army, the Church of the Nazarene, the Southern Baptist Convention, and the Latter-day Saints posted impressive gains.

Given the modest African-American population in the region, it should not be surprising that black churches have nothing approaching the role they play in the South. Historically, African-American churches account for only one out of every 25 religious adherents in New England, versus one out of every five in the South. In Connecticut, however, 8 percent of all adherents are affiliated with one of the historically African-American Protestant churches, and black churches and

Table 1.5   Number of Adherents in United States by Religious Family (NARA)

Religious Family, Rank Ordered	Percent of Adherents	Percent of Total Population	Percent of All Adherents
1. Catholic	62,035,042	22.0	37.0
2. Baptist	23,880,856	8.5	14.3
3. Historically African-Amer. Protestant	20,774,338	7.4	12.4
4. United Methodist	10,350,629	3.7	6.2
5. Other Conservative Christian	7,934,198	2.8	4.7
6. Holiness/Wesleyan/Pentecostal	7,764,756	2.8	4.6
7. Jewish	6,141,325	2.2	3.7
8. Lutheran (ECLA)	5,113,418	1.8	3.1
9. Confessional/Reformed Non-UCC Cong.	4,374,743	1.6	2.6
10. LDS (Mormon)	4,224,026	1.5	2.5
11. Presbyterian U.S.A.	3,141,566	1.1	1.9
12. Eastern Religion	2,560,243	0.9	1.5
13. Episcopalian	2,314,756	0.8	1.4
14. UCC	1,698,918	0.6	1.0
15. Muslim	1,559,294	0.6	0.9
16. Orthodox	1,449,274	0.5	0.9
17. Christians (Disciples)	1,017,784	0.4	0.6
18. Pietist/Anabaptist	698,897	0.2	0.4
19. Other Mainline Prot/Liberal Christian	418,098	0.1	0.2
Total	167,425,161	59.5	100.0
Unaffiliated	114,165,080	40.5	N/A

their preachers play a particularly important role in public life in the Hartford/Springfield area.

Along with the Catholics, another religious category that stands out in New England is the "Nones." To be sure, New Englanders are resolutely religious. Sixty-one percent of them are affiliated with one denomination or another—two percentage points above the national average. Moreover, the region has some of the most religious states in the nation. Both Massachusetts and Rhode Island are in the top 10, with roughly two out of every three residents adhering to one religious body or another, and Connecticut is not far behind. All three of these states boast more religious adherents per capita than Alabama, Mississippi, or Tennessee. Yet the region has some of the country's least religious states as well.

Maine and Vermont, with adherence rates of 36 percent and 39 percent, respectively, rank in the bottom 10. And New Hampshire is fairly evenly split between the affiliated and the unaffiliated.

"None" is an especially compelling religious option in the rural north, which in many respects replicates patterns visible in the Pacific Northwest. According to ARIS, 22 percent of Vermonters claimed "No Religion," second only to Washington's 25 percent in the national rankings. New Hampshire (17 percent), Massachusetts (16 percent), Maine (16 percent), and Rhode Island (15 percent) were all above the national average of 14 percent. According to the NARA data, more than four out of five residents in Maine's Sagadahoc and Waldo counties have no religious affiliation, and in many other outlying regions "None" is the most popular religious preference. Vermont's Orange County provides a particularly stark example of this streak of religious independence. In this overwhelmingly white and rural county the most vibrant religious group is the United Church of Christ, which claims 6 percent of the population. Only 2 percent of the population is affiliated with the Catholic Church, and 84 percent are not claimed by any religious body whatsoever.

It should be noted, however, that "no religion" does not necessarily mean "secular." Many Americans with no religious affiliation actually consider themselves to be quite spiritual. Moreover, many meditate regularly, pray, and even attend church. The rise of the "No Religion" option, in other words, may reflect, more than anything else, shifting evaluations of terms such as "religion" and "spirituality."

Religious Diversity, New England Style

Over the course of New England's history, Congregationalism and Catholicism have exerted considerable centripetal force across the region, yet New England has never been religiously homogeneous. The Puritan theology that dominated Massachusetts and Connecticut never took hold in the northern colonies of Maine, New Hampshire, and Vermont. Roger Williams's Rhode Island, of course, was widely revered (and reviled) for its policy of religious toleration.

The Congregationalists themselves suffered through a series of schisms—over the merits (and demerits) of revivalism during the Great Awakening of the 1730s and 1740s and over the divinity of Jesus and the sinfulness of humanity during the Unitarian Controversy of the first third of the nineteenth century. Still, the Puritan theology favored by Congregationalists, disseminated through sermons and tracts, schools and colleges, acted as a powerful unifying force over the region well into the nineteenth century. Harvard and Yale were both established by Congregationalists, as were Amherst, Bowdoin, Dartmouth, Middlebury, and Williams.

Real religious diversity came to the region—and the country—during what the historian William R. Hutchison has termed the "Great Diversification" of the 1830s. Before this crucial decade, Hutchison argues in *Religious Pluralism in America*, the overwhelming majority of New Englanders were English-speaking Protestants with Calvinist leanings. Beginning in the 1830s, a massive influx of immigrants from Ireland, Italy, and other parts of Western Europe radically transformed New England and the rest of the United States, setting both on a course toward cultural and religious diversity.

Although the first Jewish community in the New World was established in New York City, the community in Newport, Rhode Island, is almost as old, dating to 1658. Newport's Truro Synagogue, built in 1763, is now the nation's oldest. But the Jewish presence in colonial New England was more symbolic than substantive. That changed over the course of the nineteenth century, when a major influx of Jews into the United States gave the Jewish community in New England a considerable lift. Today Judaism has a strong presence in the region; 4.3 percent of Massachusetts residents are Jews, a figure exceeded only in New York (8.7 percent) and New Jersey (5.6 percent). Connecticut (3.2 percent) and Rhode Island (1.5 percent) also have flourishing Jewish minorities. In fact, all the New England states rank in the top half of the country when it comes to Jewish population.

In the Boston metropolitan area, Jews are the second largest religious body, far behind the Catholics but comfortably ahead of the United Church of Christ, the Episcopal Church, and the United Methodist Church. Seventy-eight percent of the counties in New England support at least one synagogue, in comparison with 25 percent of the counties throughout the nation.

Catholics, of course, came in far greater numbers than did Jews during the "Great Diversification" of the 1830s. Two centuries earlier, "no Jesuit or ecclesiastical person ordained by the authority of the pope" had been permitted to set foot in Massachusetts. During the first great immigration wave of the nineteenth century, Catholics came by the millions. Blue-blooded defenders of the old "Congregational Way" treated Catholic immigrants harshly, accusing Catholic priests of molesting young women and brainwashing young men. In 1834, an anti-Catholic mob burned a convent to the ground in Charlestown, Massachusetts. But by the time the second great immigration wave broke over New England in the 1880s and 1890s, the region had become predominantly Catholic. From that time forward, the Irish, the Italians, and the Portuguese would have as much to say about the course of New England history as the Lowells, the Cabots, and the Lodges.

Over the course of the twentieth century, Catholics gained social acceptance and political power. Rhode Island elected its first Catholic governor (James H. Higgins, a Democrat) in 1907, and Massachusetts' first Catholic governor (David Walsh, also a Democrat) came to power in 1913. Far sooner than the nation as a whole, New England became a Judeo-Christian region in which Protestants, Catholics, and Jews all commanded a corner of the public square. At least in that regard, it is fitting that the region provided, in the person of John F. Kennedy, the first Catholic elected to run the nation.

Religious diversity came to New England through home-grown initiatives as well. Transcendentalists such as Ralph Waldo Emerson and Henry David Thoreau introduced to citizens of Concord, Massachusetts, and the wider region a new form of spirituality in which divinity resided in ant hills, Asian religions, and the human heart. But Transcendentalists—the first group of American intellectuals to see truth and beauty in Asian scriptures—were not New England's only spiritual renegades in the early republic. Northern New England proved fertile soil for radical sectarians such as the Universalists, who taught that a loving God would eventually gather all His creatures, Christians and non-Christians alike, into heaven. So too for the youthful musings of Joseph Smith, the Vermont-born seeker who founded in 1830 the most successful new religious movement in American history: The Church of Jesus Christ of Latter-day Saints. Much later in the nineteenth century, Mary Baker Eddy, of Bow, New Hampshire, would establish the Church of Jesus Christ, Scientist, now headquartered in Boston. The Shakers, also inspired by a female founder (Ann Lee), maintained communities in many New England states.

More radical religious diversity came to New England in the late nineteenth century. New Englanders had first learned about Hinduism after their sea captains initiated trade with India in 1784. In 1790, there were reports of a "Hindoo" walking the streets of the port of Salem, Massachusetts, and in the 1840s an English translation of the Hindu scripture, the Bhagavad Gita, landed in the laps of Concord's Transcendentalists. But Hindu teachers did not come to the region until the 1890s.

Following the World's Parliament of Religions, which brought Hindus and Buddhists, Sikhs and Confucians to Chicago in 1893, New England became a hotbed for New World Hinduism. Swami Vivekananda, who had encamped in Boston and obtained credentials from the Harvard professor John Henry Wright before making his way to Chicago and the Parliament, returned to New England regularly thereafter. He spoke at Harvard, Radcliffe, and Smith College, and he was a regular at Green Acre, a spiritual retreat center in Eliot, Maine, founded shortly after the Parliament in an effort to keep its ecumenical spirit alive. Soon Boston was a burgeoning center of Hindu thought, led by Swami Paramananda, who oversaw the Boston Vedanta Centre (established in 1907) and edited the first Hindu magazine in the United States, the Boston-based *Message of the East*, beginning in 1912.

Boston also became a hot spot for American Buddhism, thanks to the efforts of "Boston Buddhists" such as Ernest Fenollosa and William Sturgis Bigelow, who each took the precepts of Tendai Buddhism in Japan in 1885. Inclined toward Japanese culture as much as the Buddhist religion, these literary men approached their newfound faith through art. Many of the artifacts they gathered during their years in Japan made their way into the Museum of Fine Arts in Boston which, thanks to their efforts, now houses one of the finest collections of Buddhist art in the United States.

During the 1880s, the Reverend Phillips Brooks of Boston's Trinity Church joked that "a large part of Boston prefers to consider itself Buddhist rather than Christian." In 1895, the Reverend Henry King of Providence's First Baptist Church asked, "Shall we all become Buddhists?" The answer was no, but the question testifies to the fact that a Buddhist vogue, inspired by Fenollosa, Bigelow, and other Boston Buddhists, gripped New England intellectuals during the last quarter of the nineteenth century.

Far more than the World's Parliament of Religions or the late nineteenth century Buddhist vogue, however, the Immigration Act of 1965 paved the way for the religious diversity we see in New England today. After the U.S. Congress reversed the restrictions imposed by the Chinese Exclusion Act of 1882 and the Asian Exclusion Act of 1924 (among others), immigrants flooded into the country from Asia, bringing their religious traditions with them.

The arrival of Asian religions on the American scene was most conspicuous in gurus who converged on the country during the 1960s, prompting *Life* magazine to proclaim 1968 "The Year of the Guru." Controversial groups such as the Maharishi Mahesh Yogi's Transcendental Meditation (TM) and A.C. Bhaktivedanta Swami Prabhupada's International Society for Krishna Consciousness (Hare Krishnas) had an important impact on New England religious life, particularly in the cities and around college campuses. More significant than the arrival of these gurus and their countercultural traditions, however, was the arrival of ordinary religious folk from India, China, and Vietnam, who worshiped in Sikh gurdwaras, Chinese temples, and Vietnamese-style home shrines. Unlike the high-profile countercultural groups, which provided "twice-born" baby boomers with vehicles for rebelling against their culture, these groups afforded "once-born" immigrants and their children a way to preserve their heritage (even as they adapted to American circumstances). That important project of preservation via adaptation is carried on today in Boston-area institutions such as the Jain Center of Greater Boston and the New England Sikh Study Circle.

Islam also expanded in New England thanks to the post-1965 immigration boom. Contrary to popular perception, the vast majority of the world's Muslims live outside the Middle East. (Indonesia is the largest Muslim country in the world.) So the recent immigration boom in Asian immigration has fostered the growth of American Islam as well. According to "The Mosque in America: A National Portrait" (2001), 33 percent of participants in the average U.S. mosque are South Asian, 30 percent African American, and 25 percent Arab. ARIS provides similar numbers for all U.S. Muslims: 34 percent Asian, 27 percent black, 15 percent white, 10 percent Hispanic, and 14 percent "Other."

It is not currently possible to determine just how many New Englanders practice Hinduism, Buddhism, and Islam. In fact, adherence rates for the nation as a whole are exceedingly difficult to come by. The ARIS study found just over 1 million Muslims in the United States, and another million Buddhists—in each case roughly 0.5 percent of the population. Hindus, it determined, accounted for 0.4 percent of the population: roughly 750,0000 people.

Those figures are almost certainly too low, for a variety of reasons. In the case of Buddhism, many practitioners do not believe Buddhism to be a religion. So when asked, as the ARIS protocol dictates, "What is your religion, if any?" many Buddhists no doubt answered "none." Moreover, some Buddhists called by ARIS researchers never even got to that central question, since large numbers of Buddhist immigrants, particularly from Southeast Asia, do not speak English. In fact, in New England, the household language is something other than English in 19 percent of all homes. Because ARIS conducted its research in English only, its findings exclude nearly one in every five New England households, including many households of recent immigrants from Buddhist-dominated countries of Asia.

Although there are reasons to mistrust the data on Hindus, Buddhists, and Muslims when it comes to nationwide percentages, they are useful for comparing the relative strengths of these religions in different states. According to the ARIS poll, New England has a higher percentage of Hindus and fewer Buddhists than the nation as a whole. When it comes to Islam, it is just about at the national average. While New England accounts for only 5.4 percent of the U.S. population, it is home to 6.8 percent of the nation's Hindus, 3 percent of its Buddhists, and 5.1 percent of its Muslims.

Inside New England, Buddhism is particularly strong in Vermont, which according to the Pluralism Project at Harvard University is home to 16 different Buddhist groups, including the Green Mountain Dharma Center, which promulgates the teachings of the Vietnamese Zen master and peace activist Thich Nhat Hanh, and Karmê Chöling, the Tibetan Buddhist meditation retreat center founded by the renegade monk (and doyen of the counterculture) Chögyam Trungpa Rinpoche. Buddhists represent 3 percent of all residents in three rural counties in Vermont. Boston has emerged as an important center for Buddhist publishing in the United States, with both Shambhala Publications and Wisdom Publications operating in the area.

Massachusetts is the region's hotbed for Hindus. With 20 Hindu congregations, according to NARA data, this state ranks eighth in the nation. Immigrant Hindus have gathered the resources to construct large temple complexes modeled on temples in India during the 1990s in Ashland, Massachusetts, west of Boston, and in Middletown, Connecticut. Not one Hindu congregation has yet taken up residence in Maine, New Hampshire, or Vermont.

New England's Muslim population is considerable in the urban south and negligible in the rural north. Very few Muslims reside in New Hampshire, Rhode Island, and Maine, and virtually none live in Vermont. In fact, only South Dakota has fewer Muslim residents than Vermont. Connecticut is New England's Muslim stronghold, with nine out of every 1,000 residents practicing Islam (fifth in the nation), and Massachusetts is a close second with seven out of every 1,000 (ninth nationally). According to the "Mosque in America" study, there are 23 mosques in Massachusetts and another 21 in Connecticut. The region's first was the Islamic Center of New England in Quincy, Massachusetts, dedicated in 1964 to serve Lebanese and Syrian worshipers.

Given the lure of New York and New Jersey for many U.S. Muslims, it should not be surprising that the tri-state metropolitan corridor counties of south-western Connecticut boast formidable numbers of Muslims. According to the latest NARA figures, 1.7 percent of all residents in Fairfield County are Muslims, and 1.4 percent in New Haven County. As a region, New England ranks in the middle of the pack when it comes to Islam. With an adherence rate of roughly 0.6 percent of all residents, it is well ahead of the Coastal West and Rocky Mountain West (0.2 percent each) but far behind the Muslim stronghold of the Mid-Atlantic region (1.2 percent).

Some polls have tracked "Eastern Religions" as a category, and here New England ranks in the middle of the pack, with 0.9 percent of all residents versus 2 percent in the Pacific and 0.6 percent in the South, according to the NARA data. Practitioners of eastern religions (Buddhism, Daoism, Hinduism, Sikhism, Shinto, Zoroastrianism, and the Bahá'í faith) are most numerous in Vermont (2.3 percent) and Massachusetts (1.2 percent) but negligible in the four remaining New England states. The "Eastern Religions" category is significant in a number of rural counties in Vermont and western Massachusetts. Practitioners of these faiths account for 8.1 percent of all residents in Caledonia County, 6.7 percent in Addison County, and 4.9 percent in Windham County (all in Vermont). They are also a notable presence in Franklin and Hampshire counties in western Massachusetts (3.8 percent and 3.1 percent, respectively).

Eastern religions emerge as a far more formidable force in these counties when their practitioners are weighed against other adherents rather than against the total population, in part because "Nones" seem to congregate in areas where interest in Asian religions is high. In Vermont, practitioners of eastern religions

Figure 1.6   Map of "Eastern Religions" by County for all New England

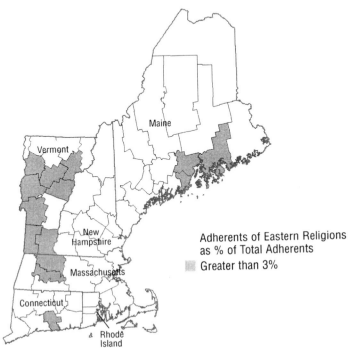

Adherents of Eastern Religions
as % of Total Adherents

Greater than 3%

account for 15.5 percent of all believers in Caledonia County, 14.9 percent in Orange City, 14.7 percent in Windham, and 14.6 percent in Addison City. Of all the religious adherents in that state, one out of 20 is affiliated with an Asian religious tradition.

Conclusion

Much has been said about the end of regionalism in the United States in general, and the demise of New England as a distinctive cultural area in particular. And there are surely signs that "Americanization" has come to New England. Like the rest of the country, the region is rapidly becoming more Hispanic, more Asian, and less white. When it comes to Protestantism, the region is mimicking national trends too, with evangelicals gaining on their mainline counterparts. Moreover, there is nothing particularly distinctive about the undeniable attraction of New Englanders to Buddhism, Hinduism, and Islam, which are doing just about as well in this region as they are in the rest of the country. Nonetheless, New England remains a distinctive religious region by virtue of its staunch

Catholicism in the urban south and its religious independence in the rural north.

Essex County, Vermont, the least populous in the region with just over 6,000 people, and Fairfield County, Connecticut, the most populous with nearly 900,000, are very different places, both demographically and religiously. Fairfield County and its "Gold Coast" are far wealthier, more urban, and more ethnically diverse. The largest religious group in Fairfield is the Catholic Church, with 49 percent of the population, but Jews (4 percent) and Muslims (2 percent) also have a notable presence in this the most southwesterly of New England counties. Three hundred miles and worlds away, in Essex County on Vermont's northern border, 78 percent claim no religious affiliation, Catholics constitute only 14 percent of the population, and there isn't a Jew or a Muslim to be seen.

To be sure, there are forces at work in the country as a whole that bear down on the residents of Essex and Fairfield alike. But the two counties remain starkly different, demographically, culturally, and religiously. New England as a whole retains its distinctiveness too. If 7-Up is the un-Cola, New England is the un-South. Like Southerners, New Englanders have a strong sense of regional identity. Yet those identities differ markedly, particularly when it comes to faith. As repelled by the Religious Right as the South is attracted to it, New England is nearly as Catholic as the South is Baptist. And while in New England, as in the South, there is evidence that regional differences are eroding, Massachusetts and its neighboring states are likely to remain distinct from Mississippi and its kin for a long, long time.

Chapter Two

Catholics I:
Majority Faith with a Minority Mindset

James M. O'Toole

In the long historical drama of religion in New England, Roman Catholicism is not the first act—or even the second or third. Indeed, it seemed in the opening scenes of the play that Catholics might not appear on stage at all. The seventeenth-century settlers who came to the place they called New England, consciously replicating (with godly improvements) the society of Old England, hoped to purge the "popish" elements they found still infecting the reformed Church of England. They wanted above all to preserve their settlement from what they considered the inevitably corrupting influence of Catholicism, which they saw as the embodiment of the biblical anti-Christ.

Massachusetts Bay and other early colonies went so far as to pass "anti-priest laws," essentially criminalizing that church in their corner of the New World. "All and every Jesuit, seminary priest, missionary or other spiritual or ecclesiastical person made or ordained by any authority, power or jurisdiction derived from the pope or see of Rome," said the Massachusetts law of 1647, "shall be deemed and accounted an incendiary and disturber of the publick peace and safety, and an enemy to the true Christian religion." Catholic priests were subversives by definition, and they were to be banished from the colony for a first offense and sentenced to death if caught trying to return. That no priest ever tested the law does not diminish the earnestness with which the colony's Puritan founders wanted to keep their people "pure" from such dangerous influences. As a result, the better part of two centuries would pass before Catholics became part of the New England religious story.

Successive waves of immigration in the nineteenth and twentieth centuries changed the dynamics of religion in New England and made these six states seem perhaps the most Catholic region in the nation, marked by an impressive institutional and cultural presence. Though the first Catholic parish in the region, Holy Cross church (later cathedral) in Boston, had been organized in 1789, that community remained a small and marginal one for several decades. Thereafter, immigration and natural increase swelled the Catholic population. Today, there are 11 dioceses in New England, each one centered in and named for the major city of the surrounding area.

For the most part, the bishop of each diocese is the final authority in managing the affairs, both spiritual and worldly, of the parishes and clergy of his territory. Priests are ordained to serve a particular diocese, usually that of their birthplace, and it is rare for them to move elsewhere. These priests vow obedience to their local bishop, who assigns them to their particular ministries. Religious sisters (usually called nuns, but more properly designated "women religious") belong to their own self-governing communities, although these cooperate with the bishop and other diocesan authorities in sustaining Church-run institutions and programs.

For lay Catholics, the primary association with the Church is not with these higher administrative structures, but rather with their local parish church, of which there are just over 1,600 in the region. This number varies constantly as new parishes open and older ones close, corresponding roughly with the movement of the Catholic population. Many parishes have schools, at the elementary and secondary level, and other entities—hospitals, charitable and social-service agencies, colleges and universities—that fill out the rest of the New England Catholic landscape.

Given this impressive institutional presence and its hierarchical structure, the Catholic Church in New England can seem monolithic, but its very size, geographic spread, and internal diversity undermine so easy a characterization. Catholicism in this region, as elsewhere, seems at first glance to be an absolute monarchy, ruled by an all-powerful king (i.e., the bishop) whose word is law for his docile and obedient subjects. In fact, the Church is more like a feudal kingdom, with many fragmented sources of authority and power, both central and local, which must constantly accommodate themselves to one another. A more realistic view of Catholicism in New England, therefore, takes into account internal diversity and differences.

What are the various paths along which Catholics have developed within the region and in comparison to other parts of the country? Is there a distinctive Catholic culture in New England? How have Catholics interacted with those of other faiths and of none? Examining several aspects of the culture of Catholicism in New England may help us understand the phenomenon in itself, in relation to the other churches of the region, and in comparison to expressions of American Catholicism elsewhere.

The Immigrant Experience and Catholic Identity

No less than in other parts of the United States, the Catholic Church in New England has been indelibly marked by the immigrant experience of the nineteenth and twentieth centuries. The overwhelming majority of immigrants to New England, especially in the early years, were Catholics. The region's ports, close to Europe, were natural landing points for the ships of passage, but New England presented both advantages and disadvantages for the newcomers. There were not the wide open stretches of farm land that attracted settlers to the Midwest and West, land that the enterprising could acquire easily and build up with their own labor. Instead, immigrants found work in the growing cities and the burgeoning light industries of the region, a circumstance that made New England Catholicism clearly a church of the urban working class. No less daunting to immigrants, the region already had well-established social, political, and religious structures, ruled by elites that were perhaps the most homogeneous ethnic population anywhere in the country.

This "native" population—no more native than the Catholic arrivals, of course, merely the product of an older immigration—traced its lineage to the seventeenth century Puritan settlers from southern and eastern England. These were the Yankees, a generalized term for Northerners in other parts of the country but in New England denoting a particular ethnic group. Themselves divided into the upper-class "Brahmins" and their less successful but more numerous cousins, the "Swamp Yankees," they were inheritors of the Puritan suspicion of Catholics, and in the early years of immigration they often made New England an inhospitable place for Catholics.

Yet, immigrant adherents of the Roman Church came and stayed in the region, often in numbers that seemed staggering to contemporaries and remain no less impressive in retrospect. Whereas only about 2,000 immigrants had come through Boston in 1820, for example, the number of new arrivals at that port skyrocketed to almost 120,000 in 1850, and close to half of those came from one country (Ireland). Other parts of New England saw similar influxes. The number of Catholics in Connecticut grew from less than 10,000 in 1840 to nearly 80,000 by 1890; between 1835 and the end of the century, Catholics in New Hampshire increased from less than 1,000 to more than 100,000. Yankee New Englanders found that they could comprehend the impact of this social change only by recourse to the language of natural disaster: immigration was a "flood" or a "tidal wave," metaphors that hardly spoke of welcome.

For all its size and social impact, Catholic immigration to New England was noticeably different from that in other parts of the country in its relative lack of diversity. For many years, the immigrant populations to New England came from a narrower range of countries than those who settled in other parts of the United

States. The Irish predominated through the early twentieth century, though the region's proximity to Quebec also meant that there were periodic influxes, especially into Maine, New Hampshire, and Vermont, of French Canadians, a group that was more uncommon elsewhere. German Catholic immigrants, by contrast, were never very numerous in New England. The Boston and Manchester dioceses each needed only a single German parish in the early twentieth century, a time when Germans were having a more decisive impact on Catholicism in cities like Buffalo, Cincinnati, Milwaukee, and even San Antonio; the Hartford diocese had six German parishes, but these were all tiny affairs, never large enough to require the services of more than a single priest. Italians and East Europeans of several nationalities were more numerous, but their presence was largely confined to particular localities. It was thus possible in many parts of New England to think of Catholic ethnicity in relatively uncomplicated terms: there were the Irish, and then there was everybody else. In other parts of the country, contending ethnic parties were more evenly matched, the outcome of internal Church conflict more unpredictable, and the passions therefore more inflamed. In New England, however, Irish dominance of the Catholic Church was never really open to question, and interethnic disputes could thus be resolved more satisfactorily. Parishes that served the needs of particular nationalities or linguistic groups could form more readily since the splintering off of these groups never seriously threatened to fragment the whole. Schismatic breakaway movements, such as the Polish National Catholic Church and the Lithuanian National Catholic Church, never garnered much support in New England, though they did maintain some scattered outposts in Connecticut.

Observers used to be able to think that immigration was a closed chapter in American history. The passage of the Johnson-Reed Act of 1924 establishing strict quotas on immigration was thought to mark the end-point for the infusion of new populations into the United States. It is clear now that that legislation represented only a brief pause in a longer and more continuous American story. With passage of the Immigration Reform Act of 1965, the doors were opened to immigrants once again, and this time the arrivals came from a more diverse list of countries. While they introduced significant numbers of non-Christians into New England for the first time, many of these immigrants also brought with them their Catholic identity.

Beginning especially in the 1980s, Catholic arrivals from Vietnam, Cambodia, and the Philippines were significant, especially in urban centers that had seen successive waves of earlier European immigrants. Older cities like Lowell and Lawrence in Massachusetts, or Bridgeport and Torrington in Connecticut, absorbed these arrivals, even as the economic bases of those cities suffered through long declines. The Church's hierarchy remained dominated by men of Irish ancestry, but Catholic officials responded to these new peoples as best they could. They tried increasingly to provide language training for priests of other ethnic backgrounds who served in these churches, for instance, to prepare them to work effectively with their parishioners. Thus, the impact of immigration and ethnicity on New England Catholicism began all over again.

Whenever they arrived, Catholic immigrants and their children demonstrated an eagerness to make their way in their new surroundings, and they did so by constructing and maintaining a widespread system of community institutions and organizations, usually centered on the local parish. Bishops, priests, and sisters were obviously religious leaders, respected for their spiritual roles. Equally important, they were also general community leaders, skilled at marshaling scarce resources to provide for the material needs of their people. Nearly every Catholic community in the region had many examples of such figures.

In Worcester, Massachusetts, for instance, Monsignor Thomas Griffin was a prototypical church "baron." Pastor of Saint John's parish in the heart of the city for several decades, he built up an enterprise that would have done credit to any captain of industry. In 1872, he opened a school for the girls of the parish, to complement the boys' school already there, and he followed this several years later by erecting a convent for the sisters who taught in them. In the meanwhile, he had built a general hospital for all the poor of the city and invited yet another order of sisters to staff it. In his spare time, he was a promoter of temperance causes and helped raise money for the Irish Land League among his parishioners.

Parochial schools such as those Griffin had built were numerous throughout New England, but they were never as common there as they were in other parts of the country, particularly the Midwest. Lay Catholic teachers and administrators (mostly women) were steadily taking over management of local public schools by the end of the nineteenth century, so building a separate Catholic educational system seemed less urgent in New England than in other regions. Even so, Church-related institutions continued to expand well into the second half of the twentieth century. This dense social and religious network was financed by relying on large numbers of small contributions (rather than the reverse), and Catholics thus succeeded in creating a little world of their own. Ordinary parishioners might live practically to adulthood without ever meeting someone who was not a member of their own religious or ethnic "tribe."

The workings of this Catholic infrastructure depended on the availability of large numbers of priests and sisters. Schools, hospitals, orphanages, and other agencies could flourish because Church personnel were plentiful and the costs of maintaining them low. From the middle of the nineteenth century to the middle of the twentieth, the decision to enter religious life was a popular one among Catholic young people, and the number of priests and nuns soared. In 1900, the

region had about 1,400 priests and 3,500 sisters; in 1965, when religious vocations hit their peak everywhere in the United States, there were almost 4,000
priests and 18,000 sisters in the six New England states.

Heeding the call, however, was a multi-dimensional process. Whatever benefits such careers might offer in the next world, they also had advantages in this
one, serving as means for upward social mobility in the second and third generations of immigrant Catholic families. In Boston, for instance, not even 10 percent
of the fathers of the priests ordained at the end of the nineteenth century and the
early years of the twentieth held white-collar jobs, but more than 30 percent of
their brothers entered the professions. Sisterhoods too were attractive in part
because they were engines of social advancement. During this period the young
women who entered the Sisters of Saint Joseph and the Sisters of Notre Dame,
two of the largest orders of teaching nuns, came from backgrounds similar to the
clergy: fathers who were mostly skilled and unskilled laborers, brothers who were
becoming lawyers, doctors, and civil servants.

Besides these cadres of workers, Church agencies could flourish because of
the way they were funded. Parish priests (unlike priests in religious orders, such
as the Jesuits and Franciscans) took no vow of poverty, but their salaries were
minimal, since their housing, food, and maintenance costs were borne by their
parishes; as a result, the regular contributions of parishioners could be devoted
mostly to the works of the Church. Sisters did vow themselves to personal poverty, so all their earnings were returned to their orders, which used them to sustain
the institutions they served. As the number of religious vocations fell off dramatically after 1965, the resulting strain forced many institutions, and eventually
some parishes, to close. The disaffection among Catholics in response to the clergy sexual abuse scandal at the beginning of the twenty-first century put further
financial pressure on the Church's religious and social services.

Amid all the signs of success, Catholic immigrants, their children, and grand-
children also experienced some enduring tensions in relation to their New
England surroundings. These were expressed most often in the form of a persistent oppositional mindset within the Catholicism of the region. Because the
Yankee population had often been overtly anti-Catholic, immigrants and their
descendants might understandably visualize the world as divided neatly into "us"
and "them." There had been enough examples of genuine bigotry—most notably
the rioting mob that destroyed a convent and school of Ursuline Sisters in
Charlestown, Massachusetts, in the summer of 1834—to sustain among Catholics
a nagging sense that they were unwelcome outsiders who always had to be on
guard against slights and disadvantage. Stories of "No Irish Need Apply" signs
remained alive long after such restrictions on employment had actually disappeared: in his 1987 memoir, U.S. House Speaker Thomas P. "Tip" O'Neill of

Massachusetts recalled seeing such signs during his youth in the 1920s, a memory that was almost certainly a false one.

By the 1960s, large numbers of Catholic voters in New England were described by one political scientist as "Al Smith Democrats": those who believed that government should help the "underdog"—and that *they* were the underdog, even after they had climbed to the top of the political and economic ladder. In the same way, in the 1980s some Catholic politicians in Massachusetts argued for state financial aid to Catholic and other religious schools. They insisted that the constitutional ban on such aid had been perpetrated by anti-Catholic "Know-Nothings" in the 1850s, though the specific provision had been added to the constitution by Catholic legislators in the 1910s. Some Catholics even responded to the first news stories about clergy sexual abuse by attributing the coverage solely to rampant anti-Catholicism among newspapers and other media outlets. The grip this sentiment had on the New England Catholic imagination was powerful. Catholics were a minority that had become the majority but still often thought of themselves as a minority.

Over the years, New England Catholics found many ways to express this oppositional mindset, sometimes subtly. When the parishioners of Boston built a new cathedral in the early 1870s, they purposely designed it on a massive scale. It covered more than 50,000 square feet, nearly as big as Notre Dame in Paris, and it had two towers soaring to 300 feet, a full 80 feet taller, its pastor liked to point out, than the city's Bunker Hill Monument, a shrine to the Yankees who had fought the American Revolution. When the Catholics of Portland, Maine, built their cathedral a few years later, they placed it on the highest point in the city. There it was readily visible, but they built it so that its front door faced away from the settled parts of town, symbolically turning their backs on a populace that had once scorned them. Edifices of this kind were not merely churches; they were editorials.

Economic and Social Structure

More significant than the plain facts of growth and diversification among New England's Catholic population was the ongoing social impact of those processes. Until the middle of the twentieth century, the Catholic Church in this region, as in other parts of the country, was an overwhelmingly working-class institution. Lacking the large Catholic farming communities of the Midwest, New England Catholicism drew its membership from the ranks of industrial workers, and for a long time from the middle and lower end of the scale of skills and wages. Many immigrants brought particular trades and skills with them, but most did not, and they had to find work in such industries as textiles, shoes, and other small-scale manufacturing, businesses that were often family-owned. Some larger firms did emerge—most notably the Amoskeag Mills of Manchester, New

Hampshire—but smaller and lighter industries (in contrast to the heavy industries of the Rust Belt) provided more opportunities for work.

Immigrants employed in such labor tenaciously retained their Catholic identity and practice. French Canadians in New England, for example, continued to be active church members in far higher numbers than their relatives who remained behind in Quebec. Moreover, this grounding of the Church in the working class proved remarkably long-lasting. In the 1950s, Boston's archbishop, Cardinal Richard Cushing, claimed that no bishop in the region could boast of parents who had gone to college, and that continued largely to be the case half a century later. The father of Bishop Richard Lennon, appointed in 2002 as the interim leader of the archdiocese of Boston following Cardinal Bernard Law's resignation in the wake of the sexual abuse scandal, had been a fireman.

As the twentieth century proceeded, however, the social transformation of New England Catholic lay people was dramatic. Playing out the stereotypical American story of upward mobility, Catholics used the institutions they had built to promote their own advancement across the generations. Church-affiliated colleges with undergraduate, graduate, and professional schools opened new paths to white-collar jobs, and Catholics eagerly took advantage of them. By 1930, one historian has written, the names of teachers in the region's public schools read like membership lists of the Ancient Order of Hibernians: Boston alone in that year had 78 Sullivans, 50 Murphys, and 37 O'Briens among its teachers. Other professions changed more slowly but no less inexorably. Boston's Ropes and Gray, one of the oldest of the Yankee "white shoe" law firms, hired its first Catholic lawyer, Edward Hanify (from Fall River by way of Holy Cross College and Harvard Law School), in 1936, and by the time he retired 50 years later he had served as the firm's managing partner. In the aftermath of World War II, the G.I. Bill accelerated these trends, opening further possibilities to second- and third-generation immigrants. When the scion of a Boston Catholic family moved into the White House in 1961, Catholic New Englanders relished his success as if it were theirs too.

Figurative movement up the social and economic scale for New England Catholics was often accompanied by physical movement out of the cities to the suburbs. Other religious and ethnic groups also fed this internal migration, of course, but the change in New England clearly corresponded to the general pattern. In central Connecticut, for example, the relative size of city and suburb switched places in the middle of the twentieth century. Two-thirds of the people in the area lived within the corporate limits of Hartford in 1950, with one-third in the suburban ring; in 1970, the percentages were almost exactly reversed. The institutions of the Catholic Church followed this population movement to the suburbs, leaving in place its urban infrastructure of churches and schools even as it built a parallel set of facilities in the surrounding towns.

Between 1950 and the end of the century, the number of parishes in the diocesan headquarter cities remained roughly constant, while the number of parishes in the outlying towns grew steadily. In the Providence diocese, for instance, the number of parishes in the city held steady, while the number of churches in the rest of the diocese (which encompasses the entire state) increased by 20 percent; in the Worcester diocese, suburban parishes increased by 35 percent. Catholicism never lost its place in the cities, especially with the arrival of newer immigrant groups, but it often faced the problem of having to maintain older church structures even as the bulk of the population capable of supporting them moved somewhere else.

Of course, suburbanization was occurring practically everywhere in America during the latter half of the twentieth century, but the experience in New England was different from that of other parts of the country. Most significantly, the Catholic move to the suburbs in this region was not a move to entirely new development tracts, carved out of open space or former farmland. There were no Leavittowns in New England. Instead, this suburbanization saw Catholics and others settling, largely unnoticed and unopposed, into preexisting towns, most of them with long histories of their own. That such a transformation was accomplished without any of the trauma that often accompanied it a century earlier was a measure of how much Catholics had come to resemble their non-Catholic neighbors. The impact of this on Catholic religious practice and, by extension, on Catholic worldview was marked. Suddenly, the local parish church was not a building one passed a dozen times a day—on the way to school, to work, to the market—a place of silent retreat where one might drop in briefly for a quick "visit" of prayer or lighting a candle. Rather, the church was now a place one intentionally got into the family car and drove to for some specific purpose and, when that had been accomplished, drove home again. Both the Church and the local parish church remained important markers of identity, but receded to a more compartmentalized place in Catholic mental geography.

Politics and Public Life

If, given the Catholic percentage of the population, New England seems a singularly Catholic region of the country, the way in which Catholics came to influence the politics of the six states has been the most visible public expression of that dominance. This did not happen all at once, of course, and it took almost three-quarters of the twentieth century before each state had elected a Catholic as governor for the first time: Rhode Island in 1906, Massachusetts in 1913, New Hampshire in 1936, Connecticut in 1940, Maine in 1954, and finally Vermont in 1972.

On the local level, the triumph of Catholic urban political machines in the first half of the century is now the stuff of legend. Figures like John "Honey Fitz"

Fitzgerald (maternal grandfather of President John F. Kennedy) and James Michael Curley in Boston embodied Catholic political success, relying on a solid electoral base and the enduring Catholic influence within the Democratic Party. These urban political machines had a distinctive character in New England, however, in that they generally remained small, fragmented, and always at odds with one another as much as with Yankee Republicans. Bosses in the cities of New England typically controlled small neighborhoods only: within those wards, each leader was supreme, but outside it he was nothing. As a result, alliances among contending factions were always necessary and constantly shifting. There was no Tammany Hall in New England; no single, all-powerful machine that dictated the behavior of lesser political players. There was no Frank Hague or Erastus Corning, able for decades to consolidate and maintain centralized control over politics in Jersey City and Albany, respectively. In New England, individual politicos were out of office at least as often as they were in, and they were constantly making and breaking alliances with one another in search of an always temporary supremacy. By the end of the twentieth century, these machines may have been losing their grip altogether. The last hold-out was probably Vincent "Buddy" Cianci, the long-time (and curiously Republican) mayor of Providence, who was finally forced from office by conviction on corruption charges in 2002.

Despite such fluidity, the Catholic impact on public policy was tenacious and cumulative. In the first half of the twentieth century, Catholics achieved sufficient numerical strength at the polls to ensure that their views were embodied in public policy, and the political influence of religious leaders might be considerable. Boston's Cardinal William O'Connell, for example, single-handedly killed an effort to establish a state lottery in Massachusetts in 1935. A bill creating the lottery was speeding through the legislature, destined for easy passage, until O'Connell's condemnation of it as immoral, "out-and-out gambling" appeared in one evening's papers; by the next afternoon, the measure had been voted down by a 4-1 margin.

In 1948, O'Connell's successor, Richard Cushing, mounted a hard-nosed, sophisticated, and successful campaign to beat back a referendum question that would have liberalized the state's birth-control laws. In Connecticut at the same time, a solid phalanx of Catholic Democrats in the state legislature, working closely with the offices of Bishop Henry O'Brien of Hartford, succeeded in blocking similar efforts in successive legislative sessions, thereby sending birth-control reformers to the courts. The resulting U. S. Supreme Court case, *Griswold v. Connecticut*, in 1965, laid the groundwork for a constitutional right to privacy that formed the core of the Court's 1973 decision in *Roe v. Wade*, which legalized abortion nationwide.

The election of John Kennedy as president of the United States in 1960 seemed like the pinnacle of political success for New England's Catholics, and so it was. Apparently settling once and for all the "Catholic question" about the religion of candidates for the presidency, Kennedy's victory signaled that Catholics had achieved full acceptance, both regionally and nationally. In reality, the triumph was more an ending than a beginning. Catholic politicians increasingly distanced themselves from positions taken by their Church's leaders and found that they often could gain significant support by doing so, especially with middle- and upper-middle-class voters.

The shifting ground of abortion politics offered the clearest evidence of these transitions. In the period immediately before the *Roe* decision, New England Catholic politicians were uniform in their opposition to expanding access to abortion. Even after *Roe*, the region's most prominent Catholic office holder, Senator Edward Kennedy of Massachusetts, was still condemning abortion as "not in accordance with the value which our civilization places on human life." Within two years he had shifted his position to that of being "personally opposed" to abortion but unwilling to "impose" that belief on others in public policy; by the time of his reelection campaign in 1996, he was condemning his Republican opponent for precisely that position, now expressing instead his full support for "a woman's right to choose"—all this in spite of his Church's unshaken opposition to abortion.

Other issues similarly distanced Catholic politicians from Church leaders. New England's Catholic bishops consistently condemned legislation to reimpose the death penalty, for instance, but Catholic legislators continued to be among capital punishment's most regular supporters. Church officials expressed strong support for the court-ordered desegregation of Boston's public schools in the 1970s, but Catholic politicos in the overwhelmingly Catholic neighborhoods of South Boston, Dorchester, and Charlestown served as the backbone of anti-busing opposition. By the beginning of the new century, the independence of Catholic politicians from Church leaders could be taken for granted. In 2002 and after in Massachusetts and New Hampshire, the most aggressive prosecutors of clergy sexual abuse and of bishops who had allowed it to continue were Catholic attorneys general, district attorneys, and in some cases judges. Earlier generations of nativists had thought that all Catholics blindly took their political marching orders from the hierarchy, but if that had ever been true it was no longer.

Beyond their positions on particular electoral issues, Catholics exerted a broader influence on public life in New England. The *de facto* responsibility for overseeing public culture, formerly the preserve of Yankee elites, fell increasingly to Catholics. The monitoring and censorship of books, stage plays, and movies had a long history, but those efforts had traditionally been the work of upper-class Yankees. An organization called the Watch and Ward Society, directed for many years by a quintessential Brahmin named Godfrey Lowell Cabot, had once given the phrase "Banned in Boston" a distinctively Yankee Protestant resonance: out-side observers such as H. L. Mencken had helped saddle the word "Puritan" with its current sense of rigid moralism, a connotation that might have surprised the actual Puritans of the seventeenth century.

Increasingly, however, the responsibility for maintaining supposedly proper public behavior fell to other hands. "The Puritan has passed," Boston's Cardinal O'Connell proclaimed in 1908, "the Catholic remains." He was alluding not merely to demographic shifts in the population, but also to the broadly based role of the Church in what social scientists call "culture-bearing." For years (until the middle 1960s) the Church-affiliated Legion of Decency, for example, published weekly lists of the movies shown in local theaters across New England, rating each one along a scale from "unobjectionable" to "condemned." The implicit threat of boycotts of those theaters that featured the latter was often sufficient to win compliance from producers and owners. The Church's ability to influence lit-erature was equally evident. In 1927 alone, for example, 68 books were banned from sale in Boston, including works of Ernest Hemingway, John Dos Passos, and Sinclair Lewis.

Beginning in the last third of the twentieth century, rapid cultural change challenged the effectiveness of the Church's positions in areas of public morali-ty. Coeducational dormitories came to New England's Catholic colleges, for example, no less than they did to other schools, and a generalized trend toward individual autonomy in moral and ethical matters characterized the opinions of Catholics no less than those of other Americans. Surveys consistently showed that Catholics were largely indistinguishable from people of other faiths (and of none) in forming their views on questions of public and private morality.

The Church's unwavering official opposition to so-called "artificial" meth-ods of birth control, for instance, quickly became a dead letter among Catholics, whose contraceptive practices mirrored those of the population at large. New England Catholics generally did not take up the fight for the preservation or restoration of traditional morality that characterized evangelical Protestants in the South or Mormons in the West. Arguments for prayer in public schools, for instance, gained little traction among most Catholics. Though Church leaders still presumed that it was part of their duty to take public positions on controversial questions, they found themselves increasingly ignored by their own parishioners, who preferred to form their own opinions. The crisis surrounding the sexual abuse of minors further undermined the moral authority of the Church hierarchy, especially among Catholics themselves. In December 2002, shortly before he was forced to resign, Boston's Cardinal Law had taken the lead among American Catholic bishops in warning against the Bush administration's plans for war with Iraq, a statement that was largely overlooked, even by those who agreed with it. The crisis risked reducing the Church's public voice to irrelevance.

Catholic Religious Culture

For Catholics themselves, the content of religious faith and the ways of expressing that faith were always more central than questions of public policy. Though it had become one important voice among many on the public stage, Catholicism was first and foremost a religion for its adherents, and they retained or abandoned their commitment to it mostly on those grounds. The Mass, the sacraments, the intimate connection of particular ceremonies with the cycles of personal and family life—these were the aspects of their church that really mattered. As with its hierarchical structure, the prescribed forms of liturgy throughout the Catholic world can make this Church seem more monolithic than it actually is.

Though the fundamental rules of Catholic worship are the same everywhere, actual religious practice varies considerably, depending on such factors as parishioners' age, gender, ethnicity, and place of residence. The practice of confession offers a telling example. According to Church teaching, all Catholics are supposed to go to confession at least once a year, and until the middle of the twentieth century most of them easily met that standard. Even so, there were subtle variations. Irish Catholics generally went more frequently (as often as once a month), while Italian, German, and Polish Catholics were more likely to content themselves with meeting the annual requirement. Since the 1960s, the practice of confession has fallen off dramatically across the board, with fewer and fewer Catholics of all kinds satisfying the minimum standard. The theological unity of Catholicism does not eradicate diverse expressions; at the same time, these differences of practice do not undermine the Church's unity.

For Catholics in New England, however, as indeed for Catholics around the world, the central event of the last century was the Second Vatican Council of 1962-1965. This gathering of bishops from around the world effected major changes in the Church's understanding of itself and, more immediately, in the way its services were conducted. The Mass and the other sacraments were now conducted in the vernacular language of the congregation rather than in Latin, a language uniformly foreign to all. Church buildings were redesigned, and greater openness to other churches and other cultures was encouraged. Historians are still debating the extent to which these changes represented a fundamental continuity or discontinuity with authentic Church traditions, but the general perception that the council initiated a revolution in the Catholic world makes it essential to consider its impact.

Catholics in New England were generally unprepared for Vatican II. Until the time of the council's opening, even the possibility of significant change in their Church was thought to range from unlikely to simply impossible. Catholics perceived themselves as having emerged from a long period of opposition and disadvantage into an era of apparent triumph, in which everything would stay the same as it had "always" been—only better. Experimentation with practices that would flourish after the council had been rare here. In the churches of the Midwest, by contrast, a "liturgical movement" had for several decades been attempting to increase participation in the Mass on the part of lay Catholics, encouraging them, for example, to recite some of the prayers normally said only by the altar boys; congregational singing and innovative rethinking of liturgical space (such as constructing "churches in the round") were not uncommon there. Little of that affected Catholicism in New England, where the Mass remained a spectacle that the congregation watched rather than something that they themselves took an active part in. The churches built in New England in the 1950s were mainly suburban copies of nineteenth-century urban models, with the people often seated at great distances from the altar and a low railing separating them from the sanctuary into which only ordained priests could venture.

Thus, when the changes of Vatican II arrived in the middle 1960s, they seemed to most New England Catholics to come out of the blue. The bishops of New England were mostly "back-benchers" in the American delegation to the council: none of them achieved the status or influence of Atlanta's archbishop, Paul Hallinan, who played an important role in the remaking of the liturgy of the Mass, or of Chicago's Cardinal Albert Meyer, who helped influence the council's changing theology. Boston's Cardinal Cushing played a minor role in shaping the document *Nostra Aetate*, the 1965 statement on the relationship between Catholics and people of other faiths, particularly Jews, but he was better remembered for complaining publicly that he could not follow the council's deliberations, which were conducted in Latin.

Once they returned home, the bishops of New England generally proceeded to implement the council's decrees faithfully but hesitantly. Only one of them, Bishop Bernard Flanagan of Worcester, did so with much enthusiasm, ordering the churches in his central Massachusetts diocese to comply with the new architectural demands of the reformed liturgy as quickly as possible.

The implementation of other reforms was spottier. Parish councils, comprised largely of lay people and sharing responsibility with the pastor for the practical management of local church affairs, did appear, but they were never as influential in practice as they might have been in theory. Pastors could, and did, ignore them whenever they wanted to. Councils of diocesan priests were similarly weak in New England, in contrast to other parts of the country (such as Chicago) where such bodies became effective voices in representing the particular interests of the clergy. Only in response to the sexual abuse crisis in 2002-2003 did an independent Priests Forum emerge in Boston, adopting a critical stance toward the actions of their archbishop and eventually helping to force his resignation. New England-area nuns were similarly absent from wider visibility in such national organizations as the Leadership Conference of Women Religious.

After some initial shocks, however, the Catholic laity in New England quietly accustomed themselves to the changes that came with Vatican II: Catholic traditionalist movements, such as that spearheaded by Long Island's Gomar DePauw, which tried to resist implementation of the new vernacular Mass, found few adherents in New England, as the region adjusted to the new forms of worship.

The religious practice of ordinary Catholics, the "men and women in the pews," changed slowly but inexorably in the aftermath of Vatican II. Going to church was quite different by the end of the twentieth century from what it had been at the beginning. Participation by New England Catholics in the Mass and the sacraments was the most evident sign of change. Though reliable statistics are hard to come by for either the earlier or later period, most estimates pegged weekly Mass attendance among self-identified Catholics at roughly 30 percent by the year 2000, down from 70 percent or higher in 1900.

For those Catholics who did continue regular practice, however, the experience of religion was changed and, in general, more intense and personal. No longer passive observers, they were now active participants in the liturgy, singing hymns and reciting responses along with the priest. Moreover, at any given Mass there were likely to be more lay people than priests taking official roles in the service, as readers, song leaders, distributors of communion, and even preachers. Rates of reception of the eucharist also skyrocketed. Whereas earlier generations of Catholics had taken the sacrament rarely (once a month was encouraged, but many Catholics felt unworthy to approach that ideal), now virtually every parishioner in attendance received communion every time he or she went to Mass.

At the same time, other long-standing religious practices disappeared, either gradually or suddenly. Paraliturgical services such as novenas (nine-day periods of special prayers and devotions, usually for particular causes), benediction (Sunday evening services that featured prayer before the exposed eucharistic host), and public recitation of the rosary (the repetition of prayers to Mary, the mother of Jesus) had once been common features of the Catholic landscape, in New England and elsewhere; by the end of the twentieth century they were rare. Some ethnic groups held on to these practices longer than others—Hispanic Catholic devotion to the rosary remained higher than that of other groups, for instance, and Italian Catholics continued to participate in summertime street *feste* in the region's cities—but these came increasingly to be seen as exotic practices more identified with ethnicity than with religion as such. The forms of religious and devotional practice had changed, but for those practices that remained and flourished a greater sense of commitment to and personal meaning for ordinary believers came to be expected. Fewer Catholics went to Sunday Mass merely to "fulfill their obligation," as the older catechisms had instructed them; now, they went because they expected the liturgy to mean something personally to them.

The Crisis of Clergy Sexual Abuse

Four decades of religious change for New England's Catholics between Vatican II and the beginning of the twenty-first century may, in some odd and ironic ways, have prepared them to absorb the repeated shocks of the public scandal of the sexual abuse of minors by Catholic priests, beginning in January 2002. So much else had challenged their Church as an institution and their own faith in it that they were perhaps more ready to confront this latest crisis than they would otherwise have been and to demand a proper response to it from their leaders. While the precise nature and extent of child sexual abuse nationwide still resists adequate documentation and understanding by social scientists, a consistent pattern seemed to emerge as the evidence of such behavior among a number of Catholic clergy in the Boston archdiocese came to light.

There had been cases of sexual abuse of minors and adolescents (mostly, but not exclusively, directed against males) by priests in other parts of the country, especially Louisiana and Texas, but the epicenter of the crisis resulting from public exposure of these cases was New England. In the diocese of Fall River, Father James Porter was the first to draw national attention, in 1992. His serial depredations on young people extended over several decades, beginning in the 1960s, before he was forced from the priesthood and eventually tried, convicted, and jailed. Bishops across the country responded to that case by drafting policies intended to identify abusers and remove them from the ministry, but it later became clear that, in many places, those policies were put into effect either imperfectly or not at all.

A decade later, the case of Father John Geoghan in the archdiocese of Boston galvanized public attention to the issue, from his conviction on a relatively minor charge to his murder by another prison inmate several months afterward. Suddenly, the floodgates were open, as public, government, and media pressure demanded that every diocese in New England (and indeed around the country) disclose how many complaints against priests had been made, who those priests are or were, and how those cases had been resolved. As of early 2004, the legal and other impacts of that process are still being played out, and the bishops and dioceses of New England remain in the eye of the storm.

The long-term impact of the crisis is still unclear, but even at this early stage some things seem apparent. Most obvious is the dramatic change in the Catholic Church's position as an institution and the degree to which it might be subject to criticism and even censure. Throughout most of the twentieth century, the power of the Church and its leaders was such that public figures and institutions were reluctant to take them on, fearful of the reaction this might bring from the faithful. Such hesitancy seemed justified by long experience. When a young politician named Maurice Tobin, running against James Michael Curley for the Boston mayoralty in 1937, cleverly created the impression in the newspapers that Cardinal O'Connell was actively supporting him, the upstart trounced the legendary Curley. For their part, newspapers throughout the region buried or downplayed stories critical of the Church, lest a word from the local bishop cause circulation to drop overnight, just as a negative rating from the Legion of Decency might cause movie screens to go dark.

The drumbeat of stories documenting the Church's mishandling of clergy sexual abuse throughout 2002 changed that dynamic, perhaps permanently, and the Church has now become fair game for investigative journalism, no less than every other powerful institution (except, of course, the press itself). The *Boston Globe* took the lead, with its year-long reporting on the situation in the archdiocese of Boston, which culminated in the *Globe* winning a Pulitzer Prize. Other factors also contributed to its doggedness in pursuing the story. A few years before the story broke, the *Globe* was sold by its local owners—a single family, the Taylors, had owned and run it for more than a century—to the *New York Times* company, which brought in a new editor from Florida. Not knowing from unspoken local tradition that he should fear the archdiocese, he never ordered his reporters to back off from the story, thereby demonstrating that harsh but honest assessments of Church leaders and policies were acceptable or even required.

Elected officials, many of them "cradle Catholics," joined in pursuing the investigation of cardinals and bishops. Thomas Reilly, Massachusetts' attorney general, a practicing Catholic who had attended Boston College Law School, issued a stinging report in the summer of 2003 detailing the history of sexual abuse in the archdiocese. His report quickly stated what everyone already knew—that, in the absence of specific statutes (such as mandated reporter laws), there were no crimes for which archdiocesan officials could be prosecuted. He went on, however, at length to blame Cardinal Law and his associates for repeated failures of "leadership." A Catholic politician criticizing his archbishop's "leadership" was something new in New England Catholicism. Now, there was not only no political downside, but perhaps many advantages, to doing so.

The impact of the scandal on lay Catholics was perhaps even more substantial. In response to the stream of reports—one Catholic observer described it as getting punched in the stomach every day, just picking up the morning paper—new forms of lay activism sprang into being. An informal group of parishioners in suburban Wellesley began meeting in their church basement in the winter of 2002 to discuss the crisis and what they should do about it; within a few weeks an organization, Voice of the Faithful (VOTF), was born, taking as its motto "Keep the faith, change the Church." It grew to claim 30,000 members nation-wide within a few months. There were limitations on the group's appeal: it was (and remains) an overwhelmingly white, middle-aged, and upper-middle-class phenomenon. Still, the idea that a permanent organization of lay people, openly critical of their bishops and pressing for structural change in the Church as a whole, would have been impossible to imagine even a few months before.

On the local parish level, the impact of the scandal in Boston and across New England has been mixed. Some parishioners found that they could simply no longer continue to call themselves Catholics in light of the obvious moral failings of the hierarchy. Weekly attendance at Mass and donations both fell off, in some places quite sharply. Special annual collections for the support of Catholic chari-ties and educational institutions found their returns substantially down.

Anecdotal evidence alone documents these trends, but in all cases the decline seems to have been far less dramatic than one might have expected. In at least one suburban Boston parish, weekly offerings actually went up for a brief time after the first disclosures, apparently because the people were directing to their own church donations they might otherwise have given to the archdiocese. In many places, parishioners angry at Cardinal Law and other bishops rallied around their own pastor: they were disaffected, perhaps permanently, from the hierarchy, but they continued to approve and support "their guy." The number of those who for-mally joined other denominations (such as the Episcopal church), though unmea-sured scientifically, seems to have been quite small. Those who considered them-selves "cradle" or "cultural" Catholics were apparently reluctant to give up those identities. Five decades of preaching and teaching since the close of the Second Vatican Council had described the Church as the "People of God": parishioners had heard repeatedly that they—not the pope, the bishops, the clergy, or sisters, but they themselves—were the Catholic Church. Apparently, they believed it.

Conclusion

Catholicism in New England has experienced many of the same successes and failings as it has in other parts of the country. Today, there are competing signs that the Catholic Church is at once thriving and in crisis. In real terms, the Catholic pop-ulation as a whole has continued to expand—not, perhaps, with the "tidal wave" proportions of the nineteenth century, but steadily enough that no other denomina-tion approaches Catholicism's primacy among the region's church-goers.

In rural New England, however, and in some of the region's de-industrializ-ing cities, Catholic numbers are beginning to fall off for the first time in more than a century. The diocese of Springfield, for example, occupying the four west-ern counties of Massachusetts, saw its Catholic population decline by almost one-quarter during the last third of the twentieth century. While Catholics grew as a percentage of the population in dioceses with substantial suburban bases (Providence and Bridgeport, in particular), decline was evident elsewhere. In New Hampshire, Catholics shrank from an estimated 37 percent of the population in 1965 to only 28 percent in 1999; in Vermont, where one in three residents had been Catholic in 1965, the number was one in four by century's end. Whether these trends will continue in the future or what the rate of return of such people to Catholic practice might be is a subject for speculation only.

The institutional infrastructure of the Church in New England has faced even more serious challenges in the period since Vatican II. The total number of parishes continued to grow in the early years, owing largely to the Catholic move to the suburbs, but the number eventually peaked and then began to decline. The archdiocese of Boston had 410 parishes when Bernard Law became its archbishop in 1984 but only 362 at the time of his resignation in 2002; the diocese of Burlington (which encompasses all of Vermont) had 99 parishes in 1965, but only 86 in 2002.

The declining number of priests has also been hard to ignore in New England, as it is everywhere in the country. Between 1965 and 2000, every diocese in New England saw its clerical labor force reduced dramatically, even as the average age of priests climbed steadily. Ordination classes of new priests from New England's only seminary for diocesan clergy (Saint John's in Brighton, Massachusetts) dropped from close to 100 men in the 1950s to single digits, bringing the replacement rate for those diocesan priests who retire, die, or leave the ministry well below the break-even point.

The declining number of religious sisters has been even more striking. The largely female labor force that had made possible the impressive network of schools and charitable agencies has been aging and disappearing before Catholics' very eyes. The diocese of Portland (which encompasses all of Maine) lost 65 percent of its nuns between 1965 and 2000, Fall River lost 64 percent, and Burlington lost 60 percent. The consequent withdrawal of sisters from many of their traditional works opened up new opportunities for lay Catholics, both women and men, as teachers and administrators, but the need to pay these new workers something approaching an adequate salary only increased the financial pressures on institutions that had traditionally operated without large endowments.

The future of Catholicism and the Catholic Church in New England is, of course, impossible to predict. More optimistic Church leaders see a return to the glory days of full seminaries and convents, if only Catholics will pray hard enough for them. The pessimistic see only institutional collapse, already well underway in many areas and intensified by the sexual abuse crisis.

Whatever proportion of optimism and pessimism proves to be justified, the reduced institutional presence of the Catholic Church in the region is already a fact. Unlike in many dioceses in the rural Midwest and West, the Church in New England may not yet have felt the full impact of priestless parishes, but that seems only a matter of time.

Among Catholics themselves, however, religious identity continues to prove remarkably tenacious. The organizing of lay groups, especially in response to the sexual abuse crisis, seems to demonstrate that lay Catholics will not easily abandon a Church they have come to think of as "theirs." However much their Church and their participation in it may change in response to future developments, Catholics do indeed "remain" in New England and will continue to do so.

CHAPTER THREE

CATHOLICS II:
IN THE FLUX OF CRISIS

Michele Dillon

"I have no hatred," boomed the large bold-face headline on the front page of the *Boston Globe* on a cold Sunday in December 2002. Beneath it, the close-up photograph of the face of a clearly perturbed Cardinal Bernard Law spoke volumes. Some readers might comment on the pastoral incongruity presented by the juxtaposition of a religious leader and the word "hatred;" the more psychoanalytically versed might point out that negation really means its inverse. Yet, the broader iconic significance of the message was unmistakable: The Cardinal archbishop of Boston, a man renowned for his close ties to national political leaders, and more importantly perhaps to the Vatican and Pope John Paul II, was in some kind of trouble. That trouble culminated in his coerced resignation in the midst of the Catholic Church's child sex abuse scandal, a scandal of institutional wrongdoing that catapulted the Church into a state of crisis for two years.

The scandal of Church sex abuse has many sites across America and around the world, tainting such thoroughly Catholic countries as Ireland and Poland. But its epicenter has been in New England, more specifically in the archdiocese of Boston. For good historical reasons we are accustomed to thinking of New England religion as Puritanism. New England, however, as so clearly highlighted by Figure 3-1, is the most densely Catholic region in the country. Catholics comprise 69 percent of all religious adherents in New England; and Massachusetts and its neighbor to the south, Rhode Island, are the region's most densely Catholic states. In New England at the beginning of the twenty-first century, the public face of religion is largely Catholic, if measured by nothing other than the

Figure 3.1   U.S. and New England Catholicism

	Catholics as Percentage of Adherents	Catholics as Percentage of Total Population
New England	68.5	42.2
Middle Atlantic	52.5	34.6
South	13.5	8.0
Midwest	39.3	23.2
Southern Crossroads	27.6	18.6
Mountain West	34.4	17.8
Pacifici Northwest	30.2	11.3
Pacific	54.5	28.7
National Average	37.0	22.0

fact that the people going to religious services on any given weekend are most likely Catholic. Given this context, the words and face of Cardinal Law amplified a new social reality: The anchoring core of the American Catholic Church, the Catholic hub that produced the first American Catholic President, was in a crisis, and a crisis of its own making.

From isolated parishes in rural Maine to the affluent suburbs of Fairfield County in Connecticut, and most especially in the region's capital, Boston, Catholics and non-Catholics alike have been forced to see a Church that many believed to have greater integrity than was revealed by the torrent of priest sex abuse cases whose details dominated the local news for months. The multifaceted issues surrounding the Church's sex abuse crisis raise many challenging topics of discussion, from the personality profile of the sexually abusive individual to the institutional structures and culture of the Catholic Church. But for those either living in, or writing about, New England, the looming question centers on what the crisis is doing or going to do to the Catholic Church and its institutional presence in New England. It is a question that necessarily overshadows this chapter.

The Institutional Structure of the Church

The structure of New England Catholicism is similar to Catholicism's structure in America as a whole, and in most other societies. It is part of a global transnational Catholic Church whose headquarters in Vatican City under the headship of the pope determines its organizational structure, its personnel, official teachings and doctrines, and its everyday practices. Within this clearly defined structure, in ascending order, are parishes, dioceses, and archdioceses. Each has its corresponding ordained executives: Priests, bishops, and archbishops. Some archbishops are also cardinals, a title whose status within the Church gives them (if they are 80 or younger) power to vote in papal elections and thus play a critical role in the reproduction and or transformation of the Catholic Church.

Although the Catholic Church is highly structured and hierarchical, the diocese or archdiocese is the principal judicial and pastoral unit, and thus the bishop or archbishop independently oversees all the varied Catholic activities in his domain. These include all of the parish ministries (including the Mass and other liturgies, education, and family and social outreach programs); specialized ministries such as the Pro-Life Office and Ethnic Apostolates; campus ministry programs in Catholic and secular colleges and universities; the teaching of Catholic theology (at Catholic and non-Catholic colleges and universities); diocesan newspapers, and television and radio stations; Catholic colleges and universities; Catholic and Catholic-affiliated hospitals; and Catholic Charities, the Church's social-services organization.

The breadth of institutional functions at issue necessarily means that diocesan officials maintain a wide array of professional and pastoral relations. Among the most important intra-church constituencies for bishops and archbishops are the religious orders that own and/or manage Catholic hospitals, other medical facilities, and colleges and universities. This institutional relation has become more complicated over time.

In the early history of New England Catholicism, the various religious orders that ran the Catholic hospitals and colleges saw themselves as part of the infrastructure of immigrant Catholicism, providing Catholics with "safe" (i.e., non-Protestant) spaces in which to be educated and healed, and additionally in the case of hospitals to receive the last sacrament when death was imminent. As a result of a confluence of social, economic, and cultural factors, these relations have shifted considerably, especially in the last three or four decades.

The increased cultural mainstreaming of Catholics, specifically their upward socio-economic mobility in the post-World-War-II period and their penetration into professional and political spheres that had been dominated by Protestants, challenged the functional necessity of having distinctly Catholic educational institutions. In the medical arena, the increased economic rationalization of hospitals and medical centers has made it advantageous for Catholic hospitals to merge with historically non-Catholic medical institutions and owners. These different developments have forced Catholic colleges and hospitals, respectively, to clarify and redefine their Catholic identity and mission, including, in many cases, their discrete identity as religious orders (e.g., Jesuits, Sisters of Mercy), a task that is ongoing.

At the same time, of course, the lessening of these institutions' confessional role and the expansion of their mission to include substantial non-Catholic populations (e.g., non-Catholic students, faculty, patients, medical professionals) means that the Catholic Church's stake in public-policy debates has significantly transcended parochial or denominational issues to include the range of secular—bureaucratic, fiscal, administrative and other—concerns confronting these sectors today. This political development may be especially far-reaching in New England (specifically the Boston archdiocese) given that it is a nationally and internationally renowned center of education and medicine.

Independent of, but not unrelated to, the new policy issues that confront the Church as a "secular" institutional provider of education, medicine, and social services, is the Church's moral-political agenda and the institutional mechanisms for its articulation. Each diocese has a public policy office that lobbies for legislation that reflects and extends Catholic teaching on various issues of concern to the Church.

Diocesan boundaries (because they are Church units determined by Rome) do not necessarily coincide with state territorial boundaries and consequently, in states with more than one diocese, it is customary (though there are exceptions) for dioceses to align as state Catholic conferences so that the Church can speak with one voice on state legislative and public policy issues.

Thus the four dioceses in Massachusetts (Boston, Worcester, Springfield, and Fall River) comprise the Massachusetts Catholic Conference, and the dioceses of Bridgeport, Hartford, and Norwich comprise the Connecticut Catholic Conference. The states' Catholic Conferences are important and well-staffed professional offices that seek to present Catholic teaching to critical decision-making bodies with the view toward effecting policy outcomes in their respective state. All the state conferences are part of the national body of bishops, the United States Catholic Conference, whose many committees and sub-committees play an influential role in articulating Catholic teaching on a range of issues to Catholics, American policy makers, and the public at large.

From a structural perspective, therefore, the Catholic Church in New England is a rather formidable force. As an employer and purchaser it contributes substantially to the local and regional economy; as an educator it speaks to many young individuals at critically formative moments in their lives; as a social-service provider and healer it provides material and spiritual nourishment to many whose lives would otherwise be impoverished; and as a moral voice it addresses diverse audiences across several local, regional, and national forums. Why then is Catholicism in New England in crisis?

Catholic Commitment and Activism in a Time of Crisis

In the current moment there are several indications that the Church is paying a high price for the institutional mistakes in its pattern of covering up the presence of sexually abusive priests. In September 2003, the new archbishop of Boston, Sean O'Malley, agreed to pay a legal settlement of $85 million to a group of more than 500 victims. Many Catholics welcomed this settlement, largely because after months of protracted negotiations it allowed the Church in some sense to turn the corner as it proceeds slowly in its attempt to rebuild the trust that was so badly squandered by Church leaders. Nonetheless, the settlement itself is costly.

It is expected that some of the money will come from the Church's insurance companies. But a substantial amount will still have to be raised by the archdiocese itself. This means that irrespective of how the Church raises the required money—by selling Church property for example, or by cutting back on some of its diocesan programs—resources that could have been directed to bolster the pastoral care and social support offered by the Church to the laity and to non-Catholics—will instead be used to pay for the "sins of the fathers," the priests and bishops whose pastoral and official roles during the scandals make them directly accountable for the Church's crisis.

Quite apart from the direct financial costs exacted by the scandal are the long-term legitimation costs incurred by the Church, and these are not so easily quantified. From an institutional perspective, there are two primary audiences—apart from the Vatican—to whom the American Church leadership seeks to speak with moral authority: the Catholic laity and the public at large, audiences that in New England have a high degree of overlap. The laity in New England have been clearly dismayed by the sex abuse crisis and have expressed this most evidently in three ways: By not attending church services as frequently as they used to; by giving less money to the Church than they previously gave; and by collectively organizing as laity with an active stake in the Church.

Consider some of the recent trends in New England Catholicism. Opinion poll data and the Church's own self-counting indicate that a substantial minority of Catholics have stopped attending church since the scandal broke. Prior to the scandal, national poll data (based on the General Social Survey, a highly respected, large-scale annual survey of religion and other topics conducted since 1972 by the National Opinion Research Center at the University of Chicago), showed that New England Catholics attended church as frequently as their co-religionists outside the region (44 percent weekly attendance). Yet, a *Boston Globe* survey conducted in May 2003 found that only 35 percent of Boston-area Catholics were then attending weekly Mass, and Church officials themselves estimated an approximate 14 percent decline in attendance. Of further note, the *Globe* poll found that 27 percent of self-identified Catholics in the Boston archdiocese said that the sex abuse scandal has caused them to attend Mass less regularly, and 18 percent said that it had made them less likely to encourage their children to practice Catholicism. Moreover, almost one in every five Boston Catholics polled said that they had considered joining a non-Catholic church during the past year.

In an April 2002 poll conducted for the *Boston Globe*, just a couple of months after the sex abuse scandal became a topic of daily conversation, almost one-third of Catholics in the Boston archdiocese said that the scandal had caused them to donate less money to the Church. In May 2003, another *Globe* poll found that 44 percent of Boston Catholics had reduced their donations from pre-scandal giving.

This decline in financial support has been confirmed by Church leaders who acknowledge that weekly and other donations have declined substantially since the scandal began. It is estimated that the Annual Cardinal's Appeal (now rebranded the Annual Catholic Appeal) declined from $16 million in 2001 to $8.8 million in 2002. And while the amount of money donated during weekly Mass collections across dioceses in the United States steadily increased in 2002, despite both the scandal and the economic downturn, the Boston archdiocese was an exception, with an estimated decline of 8 percent (according to a Harris report to the United States Conference of Catholic Bishops in November 2003).

The resistance shown by the New England Catholic laity in not attending Mass and/or reducing their financial contributions is complemented on another front, by a phenomenal increase in lay activism. Most notably, Voice of the Faithful (VOTF) was founded by a small group of lay Catholics in Wellesley, an affluent suburb of Boston, just weeks after the first stories of the sex abuse scandal broke in the media. As a barometer of the dismay, frustration, and anger felt by so many Catholics, people from all across Massachusetts, as well as from New Hampshire and Rhode Island, attended VOTF's weekly meetings right from the start and especially once word of its existence spread (primarily through Internet contacts and from extensive media coverage).

Lay activism surged and was evidenced by the exponential increases in VOTF's formal membership, as well as in the growing pains the organization itself faced in adopting formal structures and policies. At the end of 2003, VOTF had an estimated 25,000 members. It has several active chapters all across the United States, but most prominently in New England and New York, and its members appear highly committed to an ongoing program of lay education and activism aimed toward seeking specific structural changes in the Church.

Complementing the activism of VOTF, additional groups of Catholics disaffected by the Church leadership's role in the sex abuse scandal have also collectively organized. In New Hampshire, "Catholics for Moral Leadership" formed in March 2003 to specifically express outrage at what they saw as the continuing lack of accountability taken by Bishop John McCormack of Manchester (the diocese covering all of New Hampshire Catholics) and his assistant, Bishop Francis Christian, for moving abusive priests from one parish to another. This group has pressed for the resignation of both bishops and continues to speak out and to publicly protest, for example outside the Manchester Cathedral on Sunday, September 21, 2003, against the New Hampshire Church leadership.

The rise and expansion of lay activist groups, and especially of VOTF with its focused agenda for shaping change in Church structures, is testament to a new sense of empowerment among Catholic laity. Of course, Catholic lay activism in New England is not a wholly new phenomenon. In contemporary times, Vatican II affirmed the important role of the laity in guiding the Church as the "champion of human rights." Through pronouncements such as those that the laity should be given "every opportunity [to] participate in the saving work of the Church," and that they are not only permitted but *obliged* to express informed opinions on issues pertaining to the Church, Vatican II singled out the laity as having a legitimate role in ensuring that the Church remains true to its own institutional ideals, as well as promoting the common good of society as a whole. (The Catholic doctrinal legitimacy given to lay activism is discussed further in Dillon, *Catholic Identity.*)

The new institutional and doctrinal ethos established at Vatican II mobilized an extraordinary mushrooming of grassroots Catholic lay activism across the United States. And in New England, local chapters of such national organizations as Call to Action, established in the mid-1970s to push for greater equality within the Church, and Dignity, a national organization that seeks greater recognition and acceptance of gay and lesbian Catholics, have been in the forefront of efforts over the past three-and-a-half decades to create a more participatory and inclusive Church. Indeed, many important national leaders and spokespersons for these organizations have come from New England affiliates and chapters.

The current wave of lay activism taps into this tradition. But it is also distinctive on at least three counts.

1. Its institutional origins—the fact that the current activism was prompted by a crisis produced by institutional mismanagement rather than stemming from some specific doctrinal disagreement on, for example, women's ordination, celibacy, or homosexuality.
2. Its mainstream lay base—the fact that it originated from within the heart of the Church, based on the efforts of regular suburban churchgoers who insist they are not trying to change the "doctrine" of the Church but simply the way it is managed.
3. Its visibility in the media—both via its Web site and communications network, and through the coverage that stories related to the sex abuse crisis continue to receive in the region's newspapers and television news programs.

These characteristics give the current activism a legitimacy and public visibility that previous lay activist initiatives have not enjoyed. And VOTF has been smart in insisting that it is not interested in changing Church dogma, but only

Church structures. It thus seeks greater lay involvement in financial oversight, the appointment of bishops, and other administrative matters. Of course, the boundary between dogma and structure is ambiguous.

Structures partially reflect the Church's theological self-understanding and its organizational self-presentation and identity as a hierarchical institution. This understanding, in turn, has implications for how Church finances are managed, as well as for such questions as who can and who cannot be legitimate participants in the hierarchy's power structure (i.e., who can be a priest, a bishop, and a cardinal). In any case, in insisting on greater lay participation in something so mundane as financial decision-making, VOTF and other activist groups present a clear challenge to the bishops' unilateral authority to define Catholicism.

Lay activism also challenges the viability of the structures and procedures set up by the Church hierarchy itself to give the laity a governance voice following the new theology espoused during Vatican II that the Church comprised the whole "People of God," and not solely the ordained. Most notably, parish councils, at one time seen as offering lay Catholics a direct channel in parish affairs but which gradually came to be seen by many ordinary Catholics as ineffective, would seem in the current moment to have lost much of their legitimacy. Had the parish councils in the parishes that had abusive priests been informed that the assigned priests were sexual abusers, the problem might have been handled differently and in ways that would have been damaging to fewer victims and less disruptive to the Church. It is an interesting development, however, that the recent consensus from the VOTF Structural Change Working Group (SCWG), issued as a final statement on November 3, 2003, is to "work with existing structures within the local churches"—and thus to focus attention on "strengthening and giving meaning to parish pastoral councils and finance councils."

The Church's Public Voice

A greater institutional loss than that highlighted by the irrelevance of parish councils, however, is the decline in the credibility of the Church hierarchy's public voice. Especially since the early 1980s, one of the most significant cultural and institutional developments in the Church was the increased doctrinal and political power of national and state conferences of bishops. Specifically, the bishops' collegial and deliberative process in formulating and writing position papers on public-policy issues enabled the Church to carve a truly public role for itself in American culture.

The statements collectively issued by the bishops on economic equality, the nuclear arms race, and abortion gave the Church a new role and a new voice in American society. The Catholic Church moved away from being a cultural outsider in Protestant America—from its institutional origins as an immigrant, ghettoized, and ethnic church—to becoming a highly respected institutional actor in the public culture. Irrespective of whether individuals, Catholic and non-Catholic alike, agreed with any or all of its various policy stances, the Church's voice came to be an expected and respected voice in the public sphere when controversial social questions were being debated.

Some of the institutional fall-out from the sex abuse crisis can be seen in the relative silence of the bishops on public policy matters during 2002 and 2003. Two issues stand out. In keeping with the Church's thesis of a "just war," the Vatican and the United States Conference of Catholic Bishops opposed President George W. Bush's decision to invade Iraq. So deep was the Church's opposition that the Vatican sent its own emissary, a senior cardinal who was a personal friend of George Bush Sr., to privately convey Pope John Paul II's views to President Bush. And after their biannual meeting in Washington in November 2002, the bishops issued a statement explicating the Church's concerns about a war against Iraq.

Their appointed spokesman for their *Statement on Iraq*, as it so happened, was Cardinal Law, the then archbishop of Boston. While he conveyed the bishops' sentiments at a press conference, his remarks and the bishops' stance received relatively little attention in the media and little follow-through by the bishops, presumably because of Cardinal Law's reduced credibility as a Church leader. Thus, on one of the most serious moral challenges confronted by American political leaders and the public alike, the Church's voice was quite muted.

The second issue has a more regional locus. It, however, also has large-scale sociological implications. In recent years, New England has become the site of much debate over the issue of same-sex unions. The Catholic Church has long opposed same-sex sexual relations and, especially during the tenure of Pope John Paul II, the Vatican has issued several documents unambiguously condemning the immorality and sinfulness of homosexual behavior. In 2000, when the state of Vermont acknowledged the right of same-sex couples to register their relationships as civil unions, Bishop Kenneth Angell of the Burlington diocese (the diocese overseeing all Vermont Catholics), spoke out strongly opposing the legislation. His stance was in keeping with the Church's commitment to publicly articulating its views on public-policy issues that the Church sees as undermining not just Catholic teaching but public morality or the common good.

The legitimacy of same-sex unions continues to dominate public discussion in New England. In 2003, the Episcopal Diocese of New Hampshire elected an openly gay man as its bishop, a decision whose subsequent ratification and ordination by the national Episcopal Church has occasioned much consternation among American Episcopalians and Anglicans worldwide. Public attention on the issue is accentuated because the Supreme Judicial Court in Massachusetts in late 2003 ruled that the the state's constitution demands legal recognition of same-sex marriage. It further strengthened that ruling in January 2004 when it told the state legislature that a law creating same-sex civil unions would not suffice, and ordered that same-sex marriages be recognized beginning in May 2004. As of April 2004, the state legislature, meeting in Constitutional Convention, was debating a constitutional amendment banning same-sex marriage.

In view of Church teaching on homosexuality, one would expect that the region's, and especially Massachusetts,' Catholic bishops would be strong lobbyists against changing the status of marriage. Their activism on the issue, however, can be seen as a barometer of changes in the Church's credibility associated with the sex abuse crisis. In November 2001, Cardinal Law issued a directive on the matter whose tone at the time, a couple of months before the scandal was uncovered by the *Boston Globe*, seemed to be setting out an activist and confrontational political agenda for the Church on the matter. Catholics attending Mass on the Sunday of Thanksgiving weekend were canvassed to sign petitions objecting to same-sex unions.

What appeared to be the first volley in the Church's foray into the current homosexuality debate was soon, however, taken over by more urgent institutional issues. As the sex abuse scandal quickly came to dominate the Church's attention, the question of same-sex unions lost much of its salience for Church officials. Subsequently, in May 2003, the four bishops of Massachusetts issued a joint statement to pastors and the laity in which they reiterated the Church's opposition to same-sex unions and encouraged Catholics to lobby the state legislature for a constitutional amendment banning such unions.

Given the seriousness of the question before the Supreme Judicial Court, and the possibility that its decision would overturn the traditional Christian understanding of marriage, Church observers would predict a much more activist role in the hierarchy. Following the example of Catholic bishops in the U.S. abortion debate and on comparable moral questions in other Western societies (e.g., Canada, Ireland, Poland), it would be reasonable to expect the Massachusetts bishops to make a forceful effort to educate Catholics and the public at large about the Church's understanding of the centrality of heterosexual marriage as the fundamental basis of society. The initial lack of Church engagement on the issue was surely a practical consequence of the demands imposed on its institutional resources (finances and personnel) in dealing with the legal and administrative issues associated with the sex abuse scandal. It also reflected the precipitous decline in the Church hierarchy's credibility to speak about sexual morality, a point forcefully illustrated by the rather cool response with which the laity greeted the bishops' joint statement in May 2003 on gay unions.

In January 2004, however, things changed. In anticipation of the Massachusetts State Constitutional Conventions held to discuss consideration of the proposed Marriage Affirmation and Protection Amendment, Church officials stepped up their activism in remarkably visible ways. A statement on same-sex marriage issued by the Vatican's Congregation for the Doctrine of the Faith was distributed at Catholic churches in Massachusetts, and the four bishops issued individual statements on marriage and jointly through the Massachusetts Catholic Conference mailed a four-page news sheet, "Marriage in Massachusetts: Crisis and Challenge," to parishioners throughout the state. The newspaper provided specific details telling Catholics how to, and why they should, contact lawmakers and express their opposition to same-sex marriage. Paralleling these efforts, pastors in local parishes repeatedly spoke and wrote in their weekly bulletins about the Church's opposition to same-sex marriage during the spring of 2004, and in several churches a married couple addressed the congregation, before the final blessing of the Mass, about the immorality of same-sex marriage, thus ensuring that Catholics in the pews had to listen whether or not they agreed with the Church's stance on same-sex marriage, or indeed with its framing of the complex questions at issue.

The Ebb and Flow of Catholic Commitment: Signs of Institutional Renewal

In the current moment, then, New England Catholicism is in a state of flux. It is worth keeping in mind, however, that like all social phenomena, Catholicism at any given time is never as static or as concretized as it might appear. We know from previous controversies in the Catholic Church that patterns of attendance, financial giving, and the confidence expressed in Church leaders can fluctuate in response to specific institutional crises.

In recent history, for example, many Catholics expressed their disappointment with *Humanae Vitae*, Pope Paul VI's 1968 encyclical affirming the Church's opposition to artificial birth control by not going to Mass. Yet, after several years of decreased church attendance, many Catholics, for various reasons, returned to the fold. One lesson from this post-*Humanae Vitae* pattern, therefore, is that although we currently see a precipitous dip in New England Catholics' church attendance and financial giving, these trends are not necessarily irreversible. It is possible that confidence in the Church hierarchy can be restored, however tentatively, and with it, a partial reversal of some of the current downward trends.

Already, indeed, there are emerging signs of a resumption in Catholics' commitment to the Church. There were discernible increases in 2003 compared to 2002 in financial contributions to the Boston archdiocese's Annual Catholic Appeal and to its Capital Campaign. The amount was still substantially lower than was contributed in 2001 (before the scandal broke in January 2002), but it does suggest a certain slackening in Catholics' anger against the Church (as well as an uptick in the New England economy).

These upward trends are undoubtedly prompted by recent institutional changes in the Church—most specifically, the appointment of a Capuchin Franciscan monk, Sean O'Malley, as the new archbishop of Boston. His more humble pastoral style, relative to Cardinal Law and to many other bishops who appear to enjoy the social status and secular privileges that accompany their institutional Church power, suggests that his concerns are more squarely focused on serving grassroots church communities. Related to this, the less legalistic approach Archbishop O'Malley demonstrated in quickly settling the sexual abuse cases, and his appointment of a highly respected and pastorally sensitive priest-scholar, J. Bryan Hehir, as the manager of Boston Catholic Charities, helps to refocus attention on the Church's pastoral and spiritual role rather than on its corporate institutional interests.

Similarly, the enactment of the Church's formal commitment to embark on a child sex abuse educational program for both its employees and the laity may also be seen as unveiling a genuine commitment to protecting the children and families that are so critical to its institutional viability. Catholic Sunday School programs, for example, now include a segment on teaching children about inappropriate "touching behavior" by adults and ways to respond to such behavior. At the same time as Catholic laity appear to be recovering an emergent sense of trust in the Church, there is also evidence that Church officials themselves may sense that the worst of the crisis is over. The best indicator of this is the noticeable increase in the activism of Church officials in regard to same-sex marriage, discussed above. Whatever the current signs of renewed commitment and vitality in the Church, it has also been apparent for many decades now that Catholics maintain varying links to the Church even when they disagree with leaders on various issues. The current crisis may indeed dampen attendance and financial giving in marked ways over the long term. At the same time, however, although being a Catholic is not a monolithic identity (as the data in the next section highlight), it is for many an overarching identity. Therefore, despite crises of trust in the Church, Catholics are not necessarily prepared to walk away from it.

Many certainly may think about leaving, and some clearly do leave, but many persist in staying because as a "community of memory" (Robert Bellah's term). Catholicism provides them with inter-generational ties, the sacramental rituals to publicly celebrate life transitions (births, weddings, and deaths), and the anchors that give coherence to their worldviews and aspirations. Furthermore, although a trans-national tradition, most Catholics experience the Church in a very local way, and thus the local church, usually the neighborhood parish, can be sustaining even when the diocesan leadership is viewed negatively. At the height of the sex abuse crisis in April 2002 when, according to a *Boston Globe*/WBZ-TV poll, 65 percent of Boston Catholics had an unfavorable view of Cardinal Law, only 24 percent had an unfavorable view of their parish priest (a similar sentiment to that by many voters who tell pollsters they would like to throw the insiders out of Washington but then reelect their local congressional representative by a landslide margin).

Depending on the doctrinal question at issue or the events of a specific historical moment, Catholics may reject some of what the local as well as the larger Church stands for. But that does not necessarily mean that the alternatives seem any better. If we think of a closely related tradition, the Episcopal Church, it too has its controversies (as its current debate over ordained homosexuals or earlier debates about women underscore). Similarly, while some Catholics find the Unitarian-Universalist tradition attractive, others find an emptiness crystallized by the hesitancy to invoke and name the "sacred" (as emerged at the Unitarian-Universalist Association's general assembly in Boston in June 2003)—the sacred and the sacramental that is bedrock to Catholicism.

The Social Composition of New England Catholics

Quite apart from individuals' multi-layered ties to Catholicism, or the positive impact that new institutional initiatives in the Church might have on the New England laity or in re-establishing the moral voice of the Church in the public domain, it is important to keep in mind that New England Catholicism itself is not made of whole cloth. It is in fact quite diverse on a number of social variables.

Catholicism in New England, like religious participation in general across the United States, shows variation by gender: More women in New England (58 percent) than men (42 percent) self-identify as Catholics (according to the General Social Survey). There are also age differences: Catholic households in New England are more likely than Catholic households outside the region (56 percent to 48 percent) to have a member who is over 45. New England Catholics also show variation in marital status; similar to the national census figure, the majority (58 percent) are married. But highlighting the different life-course experiences that Catholics may bring to their expectations of church, 20 percent have never been married, 11 percent are widowed, and 12 percent are separated or divorced.

Another significant source of variation among New England Catholics is social class. According to the American Religious Identification Survey (ARIS) conducted in 2001, 57 percent of individuals living in households where someone was a member of the Catholic Church were college graduates.

As the sex abuse scandal highlighted, this differential in education translates into differences in income and life opportunities. Most of the sex abuse victims came from families of lower social status, and many continue to live in working-class neighborhoods. By contrast, many of the activists who took up their cause and the larger charge of trying to effect change in the Church (such as VOTF members) come from professional backgrounds and live in some of the region's most affluent communities.

One dimension on which New England Catholicism is not diverse is race. Like the racial composition of the region as a whole, most New England Catholics, almost nine of every 10, are white. Of the remainder, 6 percent are Latino, 2 percent are African American, and 3 percent are comprised of other minorities. Among non-Hispanic white Catholics, however, there is a range of ethnic backgrounds: Catholics in southern New England tend to be of Irish, Italian, French, Polish, or Portuguese heritage, and in northern New England of Irish or French-Canadian heritage. The "old-country" ethnic denominational consciousness of New England Catholics is still such that many parishes continue to affirm their heritage in their weekly bulletin, as does St. Theresa's parish in Manchester (New Hampshire)—"Rooted in the faith tradition of our Franco-American founders."

While the public face of New England Catholicism is still very much white and ethnic European, the increasing presence of immigrant Hispanic and other ethnic minorities in the region—in parts of Maine and especially in cities in Massachusetts, Rhode Island, and Connecticut—are making their imprint on New England Catholicism.

Ethnic-group tensions among Catholics eager to preserve their ancestral language and other traditions have characterized New England since at least the middle of the nineteenth century. In the Hartford diocese at the turn of the twentieth century, for example, Church officials primarily of Irish ancestry responded to the cultural desires of French Canadian and later of Italian and Polish Catholics by ensuring that Connecticut seminarians learned foreign languages, and many were sent to seminaries in Europe and Quebec for their training.

Not all new immigrants, of course, are Catholic, and not all new Catholic immigrants are of Hispanic heritage; increasing numbers of Catholics from Africa, Vietnam, and Brazil are making New England their home. It is also important to recognize that a substantial number of Hispanics, for example, who were Catholic in their home country are likely to join other (primarily Pentecostal) churches when they come to the United States.

In any case, the sources of ethnic tension between new immigrant Catholics today and established European-American Catholics are not so different to those of the late nineteenth century. Many of the conflicts revolve around collective representation, the ways in which parish members believe their traditions should be recognized in the Mass and in the liturgical calendar. Glimpses of this can be seen in tensions in Lowell (Massachusetts) between that city's expanding population of Vietnamese Catholics and its well-settled Irish adherents, or in parishes in New Haven between an expanding Latino Catholic population and long-established Italian Catholics over the Sunday Mass schedule. All are Catholic, but the styles and languages of their Catholic liturgy differ, and such hard-to-resolve questions as what saints to celebrate in church and how small but culturally significant ways in which the pluralistic strands of a global (rather than European) Catholicism are coming to life in local sites in New England.

The region's new ethnic pluralism is also evident in the annual multicultural Mass held at the Boston Cathedral; its celebration of immigrant Catholics from Ethiopia, Uganda, Nigeria, Cape Verde, the Congo, the Philippines, Haiti, Brazil, and Vietnam, among other countries; and in the recent appointment by the Hartford diocese of a native West African priest to minister to its growing Ghanaian community. That the ethnic composition of New England Catholicism is changing was very publicly highlighted in the spring of 2002 when Haitian Catholics collectively traveled by bus from their Dorchester neighborhood to the Boston cathedral to cheer Cardinal Law at the height of the sex abuse crisis.

The new immigration patterns in New England coincide with three other significant population trends: the aging of the population, the decline in the birth rate in whites, and the increased suburbanization of the population. In Maine, for example, one of the grayest states in the nation after Florida and West Virginia, the number of individuals aged 65 and over increased by almost 1.5 percent and the population aged 5 and younger declined by 4 percent between 2000 and 2002. These trends pose a multitude of challenges as to how the Church can be most effective in its various pastoral ministries and in finding the financial and personnel resources to cater to its age- and socially differentiated adherents, challenges complicated because Catholic priests too are aging and not being replaced with younger cohorts of ordained men.

The suburbanization of Catholicism, too, is associated with a shift in the production and redistribution of the Church's financial resources. The financial contributions of Catholics in affluent suburbs sustain their own parishes but also the poorer urban parishes in the diocese, as well as the extensive social welfare services provided by the Church to Catholics and non-Catholics alike. Demographic shifts more generally challenge the decision-making and diplomacy of Church officials because of the controversies that invariably surround the closure of neighborhood churches and Catholic schools, and the reconfiguration of parishes as a result of a declining and less active Catholic population. At the same time, the selectivity of inter-state migration—for example, the increased attractiveness of New Hampshire as a place of residence for young, affluent and libertarian out-of-staters—means that the social composition as well as the religious and political attitudes associated with a specific state's population will likely change. This new migration is not simply reflective of a rural-urban/suburban shift but encompasses a social class and ideological component that accentuates the increased independence or cultural entrepreneurship that is generally associated with geographic mobility.

On one hand, this migration may contribute to the increasing popularity of an individualized, de-institutionalized religion and the increased prevalence of New Age spiritual retreat centers and practices, options that tend to be more popular with individuals from higher social classes. On the other hand, among those who remain committed to institutional Catholicism, the social-class migration dynamic will likely interact with the libertarian ideology that challenges what is seen as "too much" government or Church interference in daily life. One possible scenario is that the number of Catholics who are critical of Church structures may increase and may choose to maintain their Catholic identity only if significant changes are made in those aspects of Church doctrine and structure that are fueling lay activism.

In any case, in New England as a whole the new migration patterns will likely accentuate the cultural division between the more independent, conservative northerners who tend to articulate an ethic of self-sufficiency and individual responsibility—one correlate of this is suggested by the fact that New Hampshire scores the lowest on a national index of philanthropic giving—and their more liberal southern counterparts who take a more relational view of the individual and his/her institutional and communal support structures. Although not all of the current socio-demographic trends are peculiar to New England, they will, nonetheless, work themselves out in ways that inevitably interact with New England Catholicism and, in the process, change it and how it has been customarily understood.

The Attitudes and Values of New England Catholics

In addition to the structural or social diversity that characterizes New England Catholics is the diversity in how Catholics themselves construe and express their religious identity. It is evident that although New England Catholics as a group differ from non-Catholics in the region, there is also much intra-Catholic variation. According to the issues surveys conducted in 1992, 1996, and 2000 by the Bliss Institute at the University of Akron, high-commitment Catholics (those who tend to be weekly church-goers) express quite a different set of political and social views compared to their less committed confessional peers.

Like Catholics nationwide (44 percent), New England Catholics as a whole (48 percent) are more likely to affiliate with the Democratic rather than with the Republican party. In New England, however, high-commitment Catholics (54 percent) are far more likely than low-commitment Catholics (42 percent) to say they are Democrats; and conversely, the latter are more likely than the former to identify as Republicans (33 percent versus 25 percent). Consequently, low-commitment Catholics in New England are closer politically to both low- and high-commitment Catholics outside the region than to their more highly involved Catholic neighbors. The comparatively stronger Democratic support among high-commitment Catholics in New England makes them more aligned with black Protestants (52 percent), other Christians (55 percent), and non-Christians (49 percent), than with low-commitment Catholics.

On the highly charged moral and political issue of gay rights, well over half of all New England Catholics take a liberal stance. But high-commitment Catholics (60 percent) are less likely than low-commitment Catholics (69 percent) to favor the extension of gay rights. On this issue, low-commitment Catholics are closer to non-Catholics in New England (67 percent) and to low-commitment Catholics nationwide (67 percent), while the highly committed New England Catholics are more in tune with high-commitment Catholics outside the region, 58 percent of whom favor gay rights. In view of media images of the anti-gay sentiments associated with more authoritarian forms of ethnic Catholicism, such as the South Boston St. Patrick's Day parade and its exclusion of gays, it is noteworthy that in the United States as a whole, high-commitment Catholics (58 percent) are more likely to favor gay rights than high-commitment mainline Protestants (51 percent). The inverse, however, is true in New England.

Both high-commitment Catholics (60 percent) and low-commitment Catholics (69 percent) are less likely than high-commitment mainline Protestants (73 percent) and low-commitment mainline Protestants (82 percent) to favor gay rights. But compared to evangelicals in both New England and nationwide, high-commitment Catholics are more likely than low-commitment Catholics (U.S.: 53 percent; New England: 42 percent) and especially high-commitment evangelicals (U.S: 33 percent; NE: 46 percent) to favor gay rights.

Abortion is one issue on which the division between Catholics is most apparent. Whereas almost two-thirds (62 percent) of high-commitment Catholics nationally are pro-life, this is true of only one-third (32 percent) of low-commitment Catholics nationally. New England Catholics differ somewhat from their co-religionists outside the region in that more high-commitment New England Catholics take a nuanced stance on abortion. Just over half (51 percent) express a straightforward pro-life position, and an additional 20 percent say they are moderately pro-choice. Overall, the proportion of American Catholics who are pro-life (46 percent) parallels the American population as a whole (43 percent), and, although lower than the national figure, the proportion of New England Catholics who are pro-life (35 percent) matches the pro-life sentiment of the region as a whole (32 percent).

Underscoring the solid bloc of pro-choice opinion that has characterized American Catholics since abortion was legalized in the early 1970s, an additional 29 percent of New England high-commitment Catholics, similar to the proportion of high-commitment Catholics nationwide (26 percent), are pro-choice. Low-commitment Catholics in New England (61 percent), however, are much more likely to be solidly pro-choice than low-commitment Catholics nationwide (50 percent).

There are very few differences between New England Catholics on questions of social and economic inequality. Similar proportions of high- and low-commitment Catholics in New England support universal health insurance (54 percent and 53 percent, respectively) and favor increased welfare spending (58 percent and 60 percent, respectively). New England Catholics, similar to other New Englanders, are slightly more liberal on universal health insurance than Catholics and others nationwide. For example, 53 percent of New Englanders compared to 47 percent of Americans support universal health insurance. On welfare spending, however, New England Catholics (59 percent) are more liberal than New Englanders as a whole (52 percent).

Among these socio-economic issues, one source of Catholic disagreement in New England is on the question of help for minorities. High-commitment Catholics (45 percent) are more likely than the region's low-commitment Catholics (38 percent) to support minority assistance.

Low-commitment Catholics in New England (65 percent) are more likely than high-commitment Catholics (61 percent) and New Englanders as a whole (60 percent) to favor environmental protection. It is also interesting to note that low-commitment Catholics nationwide (59 percent), are more likely than high-commitment Catholics (52 percent) and other Americans (54 percent) living outside of New England to take a pro-environmental stance.

In view of the increase in ethnic minorities in the Unites States as a whole and apparent in parts of New England, it is of interest to explore how the Catholicism of newer immigrant groups differs from that of European-Americans who have been so influential in setting the tone of New England Catholicism. The cumulative data from the General Social Survey in the United States is one reliable source that allows comparisons to be made between Hispanic and non-Hispanic white Catholics.

This survey shows that Hispanic Catholics (74 percent) are more definite about their belief in God than non-Hispanic Catholics in general (64 percent) and New England Catholics (61 percent). However, while approximately 40 percent of non-Hispanic and New England Catholics (before the crisis) go to church weekly or almost weekly, this is true of only 27 percent of Hispanic Catholics. Similarly, fewer Hispanic Catholics say grace before meals (34 percent) than non-Hispanic (47 percent) and New England (37 percent) Catholics. And while Hispanic Catholics are less likely than non-Hispanics to believe in an afterlife (68 percent versus 79 percent), similar proportions of both groups believe in heaven (64 percent and 63 percent, respectively). A relatively similar proportion of New England Catholics believes in an afterlife (77 percent), but they are less likely to believe in heaven (56 percent). Hispanic Catholics (51 percent) are also more likely than non-Hispanic (44 percent) and New England (27 percent) Catholics to read the Bible at home. Based on these patterns, therefore, it might reasonably be expected that the increasing presence of Hispanic and other ethnic minority Catholics may lead to. New England Catholicism becoming characterized by greater personal piety or spirituality and a reduced emphasis on church attendance as the marker of Catholic identity.

It is also likely that immigrant Catholics will be more supportive of official Church teachings and less inclined toward institutional and societal change than are New England and American Catholics. Although similar majorities of New England (65 percent), American (63 percent), and Hispanic (65 percent) Catholics say that it is important to follow one's own conscience in being a good Christian, Hispanic Catholics (54 percent) are more likely than New England (39 percent) and other non-Hispanic American Catholics (46 percent) to say that it is important to follow the Church's teachings in making decisions. They are also significantly more likely (48 percent) than either New England (16 percent) or other non-Hispanic American Catholics (31 percent) to rely on the Bible in their decision-making, a source that generally tends to be used to support rather than to challenge the status quo, especially on family, gender, and sexuality issues. Finally, typifying the tighter social networks traditionally associated with immigrants, another source of variation is that Hispanic Catholics (84 percent) are more likely to rely on their friends and family members' judgments in making moral decisions than are New England (71 percent) and other American (76 percent) Catholics. The greater priority given to the views of an immediate community of family and friends is likely to further curb some of the rights-oriented, individualistic tendencies in American society and to favor public polices that preserve rather than disrupt the established ways of doing things.

Conclusion: Understanding New England Catholicism

New England Catholicism is in a state of flux. Its current fluidity is in part due to the crisis set in motion by the Church's sex abuse scandal. But it is also related to the fact that the New England region is also experiencing various changes in its social structure and in the ethnic composition of its population. Because religion, and specifically Catholicism, is responsive to the changes in its social and cultural environment, we should expect that Church officials, the Catholic laity, and the public at large will construe Catholicism in different ways at different times and in different places.

In contemporary times, perhaps the most important factor to keep in mind in thinking about New England Catholics is that—as for Catholics and non-Catholics throughout America—religious identity and behavior is very much a voluntary activity. People are free in everyday life to choose whether or not to adhere to a religious tradition. Many choose Catholicism, and they do so for various, often multiple, and sometimes changing reasons. It is the tradition they know best and that anchors their identity; it is the tradition that marks their significant life events from birth to death, the multiple strands of its doctrine and theology offer them resources for spiritual growth; and it is the religion whose world view fits for various reasons with their own sense of how to be a good citizen and how they try to shape a good society.

Regardless of the reasons why people choose to be Catholic, and no matter what kind of Catholic they are—whether liberal or conservative, traditional or progressive, mystical or social activist—the most certain statement that can be offered about Catholics is that they are relatively independent and self-assured about their Catholicism. This independence comes, in part, from within Catholicism, specifically from its doctrinal emphasis on reason as the complement of faith, as well as from being an American, especially one living in the birthplace of American democracy. This does not mean that Catholics' faith and religious identity is weak, or that their confidence in the Church as an institution is weak. It means rather that in choosing to be Catholic they are also choosing how to be Catholic.

Although it is sociologically and theologically important that Catholicism is a global transnational tradition, what it means to be Catholic—to be either an ordained Church official or a lay person—is always a local matter; it is always shaped by the local geographical context. For this reason, at any given time, Catholic bishops are selective about what policy issues to focus on in the public domain and at any given time Catholic laity are selective about what aspects of the tradition to adhere to and actively engage.

The complexity of Catholicism as a doctrinal tradition, and in particular, its multiple and pluralistic strands, invariably interact with the political tone and social diversity of New England. This means that in beliefs, attitudes, and practices New England Catholics will not always be of one mind. It also means that sometimes New England Catholics will have more in common with their non-Catholic neighbors in the region than with other American Catholics. And on other occasions, New England Catholics will be in close solidarity with their fellow Catholics in the nation and around the world.

CHAPTER FOUR

PART I

MAINLINE PROTESTANTS: CUSTODIANS OF COMMUNITY

Maria Erling

New England's mainline Protestant churches represent a venerable tradition of social as well as religious leadership in the region. But the sense of prominence that still envelops them is sustained more by lingering memories than by any active feature of contemporary community life. In recent decades members of New England's mainline Protestant churches (the United Church of Christ [UCC], Episcopal, Baptist, Lutheran, Methodist, Presbyterian, and Unitarian Universalist) have become used to a kind of ghostlike invisibility in the towns and cities where they work and worship. Aside from the occasional historical commemoration, or local reporting on the difficulties faced by congregations seeking permits for building expansion or renovation from historical commissions, congregants rarely find stories about their actions in a local paper.

It often seems that to be noticed at all, these congregations must challenge or even transgress community values in some provocative way. Lutherans in northern New Sweden, Maine, made news in the spring of 2003 when an angry parishioner, alone or in concert with others, put arsenic into the Lutherans' favorite beverage, and poisoned 15 at a coffee hour. A more typical case of mainline Protestant cage-rattling took place in Jaffrey, New Hampshire, in the summer of 2002, when the United Church (UCC) announced that it would no longer allow the local Boy Scout troop to use its property.

Writers for the *Monadnock Ledger* understood the newsworthiness of the Jaffrey church's decision to exile the Boy Scouts. The congregation had deliberately entered into a familiar regional drama over sexual politics. The Boy Scouts' stated policy that gay boys and men do not honor the scout's pledge to be "morally straight," had so offended the congregation it decided that it could no longer support the scouts. The *Ledger* story that emerged from the church action in Jaffrey did a good job of communicating the congregation's longstanding commitment to tolerating and welcoming diversity. The reporter, Bethany Paquin, clearly had access to all the decision makers and freely quoted the minister of the congregation, who functioned as church spokesperson. Specifically, he connected this decision with the commitment of the United Church of Jaffrey as an "Open and Affirming Church," and this stance was explained succinctly: the Jaffrey church is one of 10 UCC churches in New Hampshire, out of 146, that has officially declared that it welcomes and affirms gay, lesbian, bisexual, and transgendered people. Local media covered the expulsion of the scouts, but failed to address the underlying dynamics of social influence, religious leadership, and community identity briefly revealed in this conflict.

Since this story about mainline Protestants was not about theology or internal denominational matters, it could commend itself to the community-minded readers in New Hampshire's Cheshire County. Here was a congregation closing its doors to the young boys of their town over a principled application of its commitment to welcoming all members of the community. And so the United Church decided to take a consistent line: If it welcomed gay, lesbian, bisexual, or transgendered people, it could no longer allow any organization that did discriminate, even the Boy Scouts, to meet in its building, use its van, or store items on its property.

Few of the *Monadnock Ledger's* readers would be likely to know much about the political and social stands of the Jaffrey church's denomination or know how to appreciate its theological reasoning. Sixty-eight percent of the citizens in the region claim no church membership at all. They would, however, find the story interesting because it put the members of a welcoming, tolerant congregation in the awkward position of banning the Boy Scouts. Readers everywhere in the region were also well aware of actions in their state, as well as in nearby Vermont, to expand and deepen the rights of groups who had once experienced social as well as political discrimination. In the articles, some of the internal workings of the denomination were introduced to readers, particularly the congregation's use of the United Church of Christ program inviting congregations to declare themselves as "Open and Affirming" to gay, lesbian, bisexual, and transgendered people.[1] The story provided a rare opportunity for the region's mostly non-church going public to get a glimpse inside the decision-making and priority-setting work of a mainline congregation and to get a sense of the "prophetic" or leadership role the congregation was seeking to play in its community.

Church people in Jaffrey and in the surrounding towns and cities of central New England would recognize other salient issues in the conflict between the congregation and Boy Scout leaders. They would understand the role that mainline Protestant congregations have historically assumed they have in the shaping of town and community life in New England. Mainline Protestants in Cheshire County, New Hampshire, might belong to several denominations—the United Church of Christ claims the largest number of congregations, followed by the United Methodist, Unitarian Universalist Association, American Baptist Church, Episcopal Church USA, and the Evangelical Lutheran Church in America—but they share a similar understanding of the role of their congregations in their towns and neighborhoods.[2] Mainline Protestants attempt to provide a civic-minded and a moderate-to-liberal religious perspective to the mix of religious voices in the New England region. They are aware of the more limited role their congregations play in contemporary New England's religious life compared with a larger presence 50 or more years ago. But a consistent stress on community involvement and building bridges, rather than on membership growth, has long characterized religious leadership in this tradition. Ministers work within their congregations and alongside other religious and community leaders to find commonalities and points of contact between and among groups rather than to advance or promote their own denomination's or congregation's peculiar identity.

New England Protestant ministers who bring the issue of homosexual rights to the forefront of their communities are not bucking their membership in doing so. Compared with their denominational counterparts in other areas of the country, New England's mainline Protestants are significantly more supportive of gay rights. They lead other denominations in their region as well. According to the National Surveys of Religion and Politics conducted by the Bliss Institute at the University of Akron, more than 73 percent of high-commitment (weekly attendees) and 81 percent of low-commitment mainline Protestants support gay rights, while less than 20 percent are conservative on this issue. According to the Bliss Institute survey, evangelical Protestants are the only religious group that voices strong opposition, about 35 percent of their low-commitment group, to extending full civil rights to gay people. Yet even for this more conservative group, the survey results indicate that in New England the pro-gay-rights constituency is greater in the first few years of the twenty-first century than the anti-gay rights group.

(These survey results predate the agitation surrounding gay marriage and the consecration of the Rev. Gene Robinson as an openly gay Episcopal bishop for the diocese of New Hampshire. More conservative opinions may have, at least for the time being, become more audible among New England's Protestants. The passion and verve of gay-rights opponents, however, eventually must face New England's traditional, level-headed, unflappable civic mindedness, and it is unlikely that a conservative movement will build much force among the region's Protestants.)

The Shape of New England's Mainline

New England's mainline denominations claim about 1.4 million adherents, or about 16 percent of the 8.6 million adherents in all religious bodies reported by the North American Religion Atlas (NARA) for the region. Collectively, mainline Protestants come in a very distant second to the dominant Roman Catholic population of 5.9 million, a fact that does much to explain their embattled sense of identity. Mainline Protestants, however, outnumber conservative Protestants by about the same ratio: in most New England states there are about three mainline Protestants for every conservative Protestant, and mainline Protestant congregations outnumber conservative Protestant congregations by at least two to one. The relative insignificance of the conservative Protestant population continues to be one of the most distinctive factors that sets New England apart from the nation's other regions.

Notable distinctions exist, however, that affect the way religious bodies relate to each other in the various sub-regions of New England. The most obvious is a major division between rural northern New England and the urbanized states of southern New England. In northern New England, mainline Protestantism encounters serious challenges as many congregations dwindle beyond the point where they can support clergy. The United Church of Christ is pioneering training programs for licensing lay leadership for northern New England's congregations in order to maintain some form of ministry in otherwise underserved areas. In the large and medium-sized cities of Massachusetts, Connecticut, and Rhode Island, the picture is mixed. Many historic downtown congregations continue to flourish, but congregations in city neighborhoods are dwindling because of inexorable population change. In the vast suburban reaches of southern New England, on the other hand, mainline churches often continue to play a vibrant and central role in community life.

Overall, there has been little institutional growth among mainline Protestants since the 1960s. This is so, at least partly, because unlike other parts of the country, New England's town form of local government meant that the new suburbs created during the post-World War II years were already served by long-established mainline congregations. Rather than planting new churches, mainline Protestants usually expanded old ones. This is a distinct contrast to the experience of conservative Protestants in the region, where many new congregations have been planted since the 1950s in expanding suburban areas and in urban immigrant neighborhoods. As residential patterns have changed, and as the population has become more dependent on automobiles, the location of older mainline congregations in city and town centers, where expansion opportunities and parking facilities are limited, has negatively affected their ability to grow. In recent decades, New England's mainline Protestants have largely responded to demographic change by reorienting and re-imagining ways in which their existing buildings and facilities can function in changing social environments.

A good example of this conscious strategy can be found at the First Congregational Church in South Portland, Maine, which is also an Open and Affirming congregation and states that its mission as a community is:

1. To Worship God as made known in the Scriptures, as revealed in Jesus Christ, and as encountered through the Spirit;
2. To Serve our members, our community and our world, working in faithful witness toward justice and peace for all people;
3. To Educate people of all ages toward a deeper understanding of their individual faith pilgrimage, their relationship with others, and their responsibilities as stewards of God's created order;
4. To Grow in fellowship as the Body of Christ, inviting others to share in the Good News of God's love. [3]

Mainline Protestants often use mission statements to organize and communicate the congregation's key values and purposes. Typically, a congregation's mission statement is developed through a process of congregation-wide consultation using retreats, workshops, consultants, and congregational meetings to design and refine its principles and values. While the use of a mission statement borrows self-consciously from similar practices in business, an examination of the declarations does reveal distinctive theological and faith commitments that to an informed observer indicates how this particular congregation departs from the older evangelical understanding of a congregation's role to lead individual believers to make a decision for Christ. The focus on service, education, and working for justice and peace for all people keeps members focused on the world and community around them rather than on their own personal spiritual status. Even in stating a mission to educate people as to their own individual faith pilgrimage, the congregation places this pilgrimage squarely in the tradition of social service. This pilgrimage is in relationship with others and tending toward stewardship of "God's created order."

While most congregations of the United Church of Christ may have left behind a tradition of evangelical rigor, they have ardently maintained a tradition of civic-minded responsibility for their communities. They have inherited the stewardship of buildings and traditions that hark back to the founding of European settlement in New England. Congregational churches lost establishment status at the beginning of the nineteenth century—the last holdout was Massachusetts, where disestablishment occurred in 1833—but the vestiges of that privilege and influence endured for more than a century. With buildings located in the most prominent locations in the center of town and members deeply involved in local decision-making, these churches visibly and symbolically held a great portion of the local social and cultural capital. Those who today serve or minister in one of these "congregations on the green" still feel a sense of responsibility for this heritage of community leadership. When congregations are in a "prominent position" in town, it "keeps us visible, and becomes the spiritual place to turn to for many people in the community," says Rev. David Taylor, pastor of the 300-year-old First Church of Christ (UCC) in Glastonbury, an affluent suburb of Hartford.

This proximity to the center of a town's commercial and social life alone would probably be enough to keep such congregations afloat, but the sense of obligation to a heritage of service and involvement goes even deeper. What Rev. Taylor aims for in leading an "on the green" congregation is "the shaping, growing, nurturing and building of a community, faith family, that welcomes and embraces and engages all ages." This may seem only to indicate an open-hearted welcoming policy on the part of a typical minister, but the practical and humdrum focus on community is also indicative of a deeper commitment to shaping and influencing a wider social environment.

The work of "mixing people up and showing them how they can nurture and support each other" honors in the here and now the fundamental theological commitments pioneered by the early puritan ministers who founded New England's towns and built their meetinghouses. What we now call churches were then called meetinghouses, because there was a clear recognition that the minister had responsibility not only for the believers in the community but also for all the rest who were expected to attend services. The experience of early settlers—that the local congregation emerged and took shape around the struggle of individuals to find religious solace—resonates in very strong ways with the vision and experience of contemporary ministers who draw on this early history to develop a rationale for a more open approach to their surroundings.

Modern faith statements of New England's Protestant congregations often reflect the fundamental idea of "covenanting," a concept that refers to a contract binding believers into a worshiping and God-fearing community. The concept functions today to articulate a deeper theological meaning for the fellowship and common purpose existing in congregations. Ministers can use the covenant concept to articulate how the community-building work they do creates a strong connection to generations before them. Members working on projects and volunteering on committees experience nurture and support from fellow members, and this experience of coming together in a congregation can also hold a deeper significance. Rev. Taylor in Glastonbury describes the goal of this kind of community-focused ministry as bringing people to "truly feel a spirit moving, a community coming into being, and it is a spiritual experience. And then, so strengthened, but even as the community is taking shape and growing, it is capable of significant involvement and shaping of the society around it." The point of his internal work in the congregation is not only to create a jovial fellowship, but also to teach and show worshipers and members that there is a strength in this institution that maybe isn't what it was in its glory days, but can still be a force for the common good. For New England's mainline Protestants, civic responsibility and leadership is, therefore, a core religious value.

The modest goals of local influence Taylor focuses on repeat in a new day similar efforts and approaches used by ministers in New England's oldest denomination, and the public visibility of mainline congregations creates many opportunities for entering into the broader community discussion. The people of the United Church in Jaffrey, similarly acting as stewards of their congregation's involvement in their community, have together made a decision about how they will welcome others, and by implication what kind of community they hope for within the town.

Prominent Position but Diminished Resources

Despite the generations of leadership that local congregations have provided for cities and towns in New England, church people in all the denominations that make up the mainline cluster of more liberal to moderate denominations realize that their position of leadership in their towns is by no means secure or even stable. Readers of local papers in the northern New England states of Vermont, New Hampshire, and Maine live in one of the least churched regions of the country, where in many places well over half the population claims no religious affiliation at all. In Cheshire County, where the readers of the *Monadnock Ledger* live, 68.4 percent of residents are either unaffiliated or uncounted by churches, synagogues, or other faith groups. In more recent studies, writers use the term "seculars" or "Nones" to describe this group.[4]

Secular and None have the advantage of being more neutral descriptions of an individual. They may imply a deliberate choice to become less religious. Unaffiliated and unchurched, on the other hand, have the advantage of being familiar and widely used by church leaders.

In urban areas of New England the term secular would indeed describe a contingent of the population that has set aside church preferences. The reality in northern and rural sections of the region is one of a shortage of religious leadership and consequently a lack of choice for religious affiliation. Mainline denominations like the United Church of Christ have less competition in the northern counties of New England, but rural poverty and a lack of robust social structures create a diminished religious culture as well. In the northern and more rural counties, like Cheshire County in New Hampshire, or the more extreme example of Aroostook County in northern Maine, denominational leaders have a hard time finding ministerial candidates to serve these remote and economically depressed areas.

The Evangelical Lutheran Church in America (ELCA) has three congregations in Northern Maine founded by Swedish immigrants who were literally recruited in the 1870s by Maine's political (and Protestant) state officials. The Lutheran, as well as the additional Congregational and Baptist, congregations begun by these immigrants once served as the desired buffers against Roman Catholic migration from Canada. Today, congregations in this northern tier of New England have a difficult future, and residents there certainly do not enjoy the same kind of encouragement they once obtained from the state.

Mainline Protestant denominations in rural and northern sections of New England have inherited responsibility for a territory that once had sufficient economic vitality to support lively ministry and a mix of social institutions. Congregations founded generations ago still have a presence in the community, but they cannot claim the members and financial support necessary to maintain a full-time pastor. It is typical for a minister to work half-time in the congregation, and supplement a pastoral salary by working in the community. Lutheran congregations in northern Maine have done what many other churches have done and yoked their ministries together. The process of convincing congregations to give up their desire for a full-time pastor and to link up with a neighboring congregation is quite difficult. One dimension of the arsenic poisoning in northern Maine that was not covered by the media was the actual difficulty these congregations faced in calling a new pastor to assume ministerial duties. The congregations directly affected, Gustaf Adolph in New Sweden and Trinity in Stockholm, had long experienced internal conflict over dwindling numbers, and denominational leaders had the job of sharing the hard monetary figures with them that indicated the gap between what they could raise and what was needed for supporting a minister's pay and benefits.[5]

Ministry in the far northern corner of Maine has been a daunting prospect for a long time: Lutheran bishops tell stories about the struggle to find candidates willing to serve in this post. One leader in the 1950s quipped that the problem could perhaps be solved by locking all of New England's Lutheran pastors in a room until someone volunteered to go up there. Lutheran bishops today do not have the same kind of command over their ministers, and they cannot afford to joke about the matter any longer. The current bishop, Margaret Payne, flew up to New Sweden to provide pastoral care to this congregation after the coffee-hour poisoning and recognized that significant pastoral experience would be necessary to work through all the grief and anger resulting from the incident. These marginally viable posts, however, if they can afford a pastor at all, will usually get a newly minted seminary graduate. Supplying this far-flung region with ministers has been difficult for a long time, but now with fewer congregations in all of the denominations able to support a pastor, the increasing isolation professional leaders experience there makes recruitment all the harder. Denominational leaders are responding to this ministerial shortage by yoking congregations into cooperative parishes where one minister might be assisted by lay ministry assistants, who may serve without pay, or on a very part-time basis.

One factor making recruitment especially difficult for bishops, conference presidents, superintendents, and other leaders in New England's mainline Protestant denominations is a clergy shortage. In the latest round of assignments of newly graduated seminarians by the Evangelical Lutheran Church in America, about one third of the requests from bishops for candidates could be honored. The national shortage is felt especially in rural and small-town ministries like those in northern Maine. Dwindling congregations in rural areas can become too small to pay the increasing cost of hiring a full-time minister. The cumulative effect of a shrinking population, closing businesses, and industrial relocation make the prospects for these communities very bleak. The industrial era that brought so many immigrants to factory towns and cities long ago altered the traditional landscape of village and farm. The recent information revolution concentrated growth in suburban belts around university centers in Boston and New York, further isolating rural and small-town populations from the economic mainstream. The implications of these economic and cultural transformations are deeply felt by churches and populations outside of the growth areas.[6]

The situation in New England's large cities is more complex. Most of them continue to have strong "downtown" congregations, often with roots dating back hundreds of years. Congregations like King's Chapel (Unitarian-Universalist), Trinity Episcopal Church, and Old South Church (UCC) in Boston remain vibrant institutions with large memberships, big staffs, and rich cultural and educational programs. Some "downtown" churches like Hartford's Asylum Hill Congregational Church have even bounced back in recent decades, and now attract a large contingent of prosperous suburbanites who choose to belong to a congregation that is actively committed to addressing the needs of Hartford's desperately poor urban neighborhoods. Asylum Hill has, for example, "adopted" a nearby elementary school and now guarantees financial support to graduates of West Middle School who go on to college. In addition, many downtown mainline churches can draw on substantial endowments to supplement their budgets, thus magnifying the impact of small contemporary memberships.

Yet many mainline congregations in city neighborhoods do teeter on the brink of extinction. In March 2003, for example, Emmanuel Episcopal Church in

Stamford, Connecticut, decided to give up a 20-year struggle to survive. Down to 22 pledging members, a third of its congregation was over 75. In the past decade, the Episcopal Diocese of Connecticut has closed or merged six congregations in old mill towns or in the core neighborhoods of the state's cities.

In the first decade of the twenty-first century, most of the strongest mainline congregations serve in the suburbs of southern New England, especially in Massachusetts and Connecticut. Scores of very successful congregations continue to play long-established leadership roles. But even in New England's affluent suburbs, challenges present themselves. Center Church (UCC) in Manchester, Connecticut, has lost significant lay leadership as congregants move away to other, more affluent suburbs in the Hartford region. Until recently, Manchester, a Hartford suburb of 55,000, had a complex class composition and a semi-independent existence in the region based on its history as a silk manufacturing town. But as the Hartford region segments ever more thoroughly by race and income, Manchester has had trouble holding onto its old elite.

The Disproportionate Mainline Presence

The struggle against demographic change is nothing new for New England's mainline Protestants, who have had almost 150 years experience with swimming against the tide of immigration. Of those who claim a religious affiliation on the 2000 census, by far the largest single group of churchgoers in New England is Roman Catholic. Since the middle part of the nineteenth century, in fact, New England's Protestants have not been the numerically dominant religious group. Especially in the region's cities and mill towns, immigrants from Europe and French Canada, overwhelmingly Roman Catholic, transformed the religious demography of the region and made the historic Protestant churches a minority group.

Despite this decisive shift, New England Protestants continue to dominate the landscape. Their relative numbers may be much reduced from the days of a homogeneous "Yankee" New England, but they still control a disproportionate number of the region's religious buildings, and a striking visible presence on the landscape is the mainline's important and continuing strength. In Hampshire County, in western Massachusetts, for instance, where 62 percent of the population is unaffiliated, only 3.4 percent claim membership in the United Church of Christ while another 3.4 percent belong to other mainline denominations. Roman Catholics represent 23 percent of the population. But the United Church of Christ has 27 percent of congregations while the Roman Catholic Church, where parishes typically have much larger membership, has 22 percent. There are, in addition, another 22 percent of congregations for other mainline Protestant congregations, while the balance of worship places, 29 percent, are divided among conservative or evangelical Christians, Mormons, Jews, Orthodox Christians, and members of Eastern religions.

Mainline Protestant parishes are clearly smaller than those of other groups and especially smaller than Roman Catholic parishes, which average about 3,000 members in New England. One could easily conclude that mainline congregations and their ministers must have less influence than larger congregations and their ministers. The physical presence these denominations are able to maintain in more remote and rural areas, however, provides a particular and influential resource for communities that would otherwise have very few common meeting spaces. The large number of congregations in proportion to membership numbers also means that in the more rural and small-town areas of New England, Protestants have a greater number of clergy providing leadership in any given community than their numbers in the community might indicate. Catholic priests, who have responsibility for far more congregants than their Protestant counterparts, correspondingly have less time available for community involvement.

Areas of New England that are more urban, by contrast, can offer greater religious choice to residents. In Fairfield County, Connecticut, the United Church of Christ claims a membership equal to that of rural Hampshire County, Massachusetts in relation to the number of total residents in the county—2.9 percent. However, in Fairfield County the denomination has only 9 percent of the congregations in a county with much greater religious diversity than in rural Massachusetts. This diversity means that even when congregations of the other mainline denominations are added to the UCC total, mainline congregations together only make up about a third of the total number of congregations, while their membership figures amount to only 10 percent of religious adherents.

In the old industrial centers in New England, Roman Catholics make up more than half of the population of churchgoers. Protestant mainline congregations have not had the membership numbers to justify the role of social leadership that their ministers have assumed for quite some time, so other factors and strategies must be investigated to account for the continuing, if modest, visibility that ministers and congregations enjoy in the region.

An additional continuing source of mainline Protestant strength in New England is its human capital, and perhaps especially the large number of well-educated clergy, many of whom now begin their ministries in middle age after considerable professional experience in business, government, or the non-profit sector. This strength is nurtured by the presence of many of the nation's most important mainline seminaries.

Boston remains one of the world's most important centers of training for Christian ministry, with major mainline seminaries at Harvard and Boston University, and denominational seminaries including Andover Newton, a joint

Figure 4.1 Affiliations of Hampshire County, Massachusetts Religious Congregations

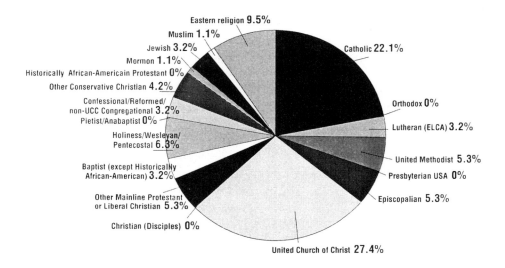

UCC-American Baptist institution, and the Episcopal Divinity School in Cambridge. In Connecticut, Yale Divinity School, together with the Episcopal Berkeley Divinity School, remains an important center of education for mainline clergy. Hartford Seminary has evolved into an interfaith institution that puts emphasis on education for laity, continuing education for clergy, and theological training for African-American and Latino churches that are often led by ministers without formal theological educations. In Maine, Bangor Theological Seminary, a UCC institution, has focused its mission on training clergy and other leaders for the circumstances of rural northern New England.

Ecumenical Strategies to Give Protestants a United Front

Mainline congregations see themselves as primarily local institutions that are dedicated to issues touching the people close to home. When the relative number of mainline Protestants began to decline at the end of the nineteenth century, especially in urban areas, Protestant leaders began to cooperate with one another to counter the surging and monolithic presence of Roman Catholicism. Social prestige was certainly one factor that motivated them; theological, or specifical-

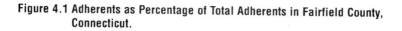

Figure 4.1 Adherents as Percentage of Total Adherents in Fairfield County, Connecticut.

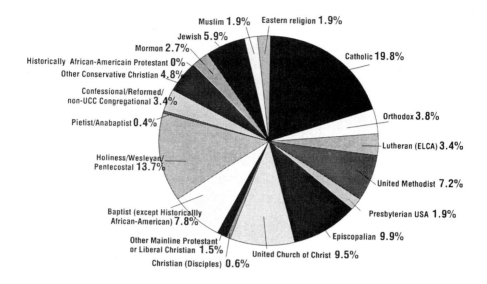

Muslim 1.9%   Eastern religion 1.9%
Jewish 5.9%
Mormon 2.7%
Historically African-Americain Protestant 0%
Other Conservative Christian 4.8%
Confessional/Reformed/ non-UCC Congregational 3.4%
Pietist/Anabaptist 0.4%
Holiness/Wesleyan/ Pentecostal 13.7%
Baptist (except Historicallly African-American) 7.8%
Other Mainline Protestant or Liberal Christian 1.5%
Christian (Disciples) 0.6%
United Church of Christ 9.5%
Episcopalian 9.9%
Presbyterian USA 1.9%
United Methodist 7.2%
Lutheran (ELCA) 3.4%
Orthodox 3.8%
Catholic 19.8%

ly religious, reasons also explain the impulse among Protestant leaders to unite their energies and work cooperatively.

First among these religious reasons was dismay over the fragmentation among churches that Protestantism as a whole presented against a more unified Roman Catholicism. The inefficiency of multiple and redundant missionary efforts, as well as a deeper commitment to social work on the part of churches, were twin factors that prodded church leaders to work for a more recognizable unity among Protestant Christians. Mainline Protestants led in forming the ecumenical movement, an effort that began with the coordination of missionary policy in the early part of the twentieth century, and developed after World War II into formal relationships and theological agreements among churches. This cooperative impulse is alive today and functions at two levels: the level of the formal ecumenical, and in neighborhoods where mainline congregations often form collaborative programs to address important issues and needs.

Immediately after World War II, theologians and churchmen from America's mainline Protestant denominations led in fashioning the constitution for the World Council of Churches; these new relationships among world churches paralleled efforts on the diplomatic front that formed the United Nations. Significantly, the work to shape an international network of relationships also provided a structure in advance of the de-colonization of Africa, Asia, and Latin America that assisted "parent" churches in their attempts to form new partnership relationships with formerly dependent "daughter" churches in mission areas. American churches led the way in fostering new systems of communication and support during the dismantling of colonial relationships and provided important models for international cooperation. In America these efforts to create councils of churches and to coordinate international church aid made visible for members of congregations a greatly expanded network of common endeavor.

Enthusiasm for ecumenism as a movement toward church unity was especially high in New England. Protestant churches in Massachusetts had pioneered in founding the Massachusetts Council of Churches in 1902. This council model, uniting multiple partners in a federated form of common deliberation and action, served after World War II to inspire churches in other states to copy the model and create their own state councils. Church leaders participated in deliberations and selected representatives among their membership who, as official denominational representatives, attempted to get to know each other and to foster ways for the region's mainline Protestants to speak with a common voice in the public arena. While church leaders recognized in each other a measure of agreement in faith, as well as a common commitment to fostering civic involvement, experience with New England's participatory town-meeting style of local governance prepared them to organize for concerted action while retaining a degree of autonomy. Known today as conciliar ecumenism, New England's pioneering form of ecumenical involvement is lay and activist oriented, and directly affected by the social and institutional concerns of the local community.

New England Protestantism's characteristic emphasis on relationship and covenant is reflected in this conciliar approach to church unity. When churches covenant to build supportive relationships, these structures can reflect more readily their local context. The director of the Massachusetts Council of Churches recently described the idea of churches in council this way: "They are far more than a thing, or structure alongside the churches. They are a *covenantal relationship*, seeking full visible unity."[7] Whether celebrating a century of service, as has the Massachusetts Council of Churches, or a more modest half-century anniversary as did the New Hampshire Council of Churches in 1999, these anniversaries have become moments for articulating and reasserting the need for work toward church unity.

The work of councils of churches across New England creates the medium through which individual churches can together advocate for issues of concern to them in the public, political realm. New Hampshire Council of Churches members met during the late 1990s to study and support legislation aimed at promoting child safety, expanding the state-funded prison ministry to include a chaplain for women inmates, and working to fight legislation introducing casino gambling. Members heard reports from Portsmouth's clergy association about a statement they wrote to condemn hate crimes in their city. Churches in the council disagreed on whether they should support a local evangelical campaign called a March for Jesus, an initiative introduced by representatives from the United Methodist Church. The lack of willingness to go on record for this more evangelical effort revealed tensions within the council on the appropriate strategy to use in order to broaden the base of support for the council among churches in the state.

Going Interfaith?

During 1998 and 1999 the New Hampshire Council of Churches executive board debated whether the proper approach for growth would be to approach non-Christian groups, such as Jewish and Ba'hai congregations, which would turn the council into an interfaith group, or to instead expand support by inviting evangelical or other conservative Christian churches into membership. New England's evangelical churches tend to be independent and view ecumenical ties as a distraction from their church-growth and faith-advancement goals. Rather than consider membership in the Council of Churches in New Hampshire, they are more likely to attend workshops and use consultants identified by the New England organization called *Vision New England,* the successor to the Evangelical Association of New England, which is devoted to serving the more immediate concerns of evangelical churches. "We want to help surface the best practices of ministries in New England to help grow healthy and balanced churches," Steven Macchia, president of Vision New England, wrote in the summer 2002 edition of the organization's newsletter. Ecumenically minded churches committed to theological and practical reflection on a statewide or national level do not share the same goals as evangelical churches interested in new methods of church growth.

Those who propose that the ecumenical movement should give way to a broader interfaith focus muster a good deal of enthusiasm among members of local churches, who realize that their communities have become much more diverse over the past generation. Others propose that mainline denominations should seek to involve the evangelical churches in order to expand their ecumenical work. The program and staff of statewide councils were reduced significantly over the last two decades of the twentieth century as denominations that historically supported such work faced limited resources.

During the New Hampshire Council of Churches' rather prolonged and unresolved series of discussions over pursuing the alternatives of interfaith partnerships or inviting evangelical churches into membership, an underlying financial reality affecting leaders was the fact that two denominations, the American Baptist and United Methodist, had consolidated their New England offices. Executive staff had been the participants most involved in ecumenical work, but now, because of the reorganization, those who had once worked primarily in one state were now responsible for a much larger area. As denominations scaled back support for staffing, funding for ecumenical work was also less certain.[8] While New Hampshire's Protestant ecumenists worried about the future of their Council of Churches, however, representatives from the Orthodox Church began to participate in the council and brought to the meetings their church's theological reflections on Christian identity. The way forward for ecumenical relationships in New Hampshire seemed not to follow the usual Protestant paths.

The urge to expand ecumenical work to include new partners is in part a search for increased financial support. Interfaith councils are increasingly being formed in cities and towns where leaders of churches, synagogues, mosques, and reading rooms have local representation that can be identified. These local efforts may seem to be the obvious next step for ecumenical/interfaith work on the statewide or even regional level. But equivalent structures to denominations do not exist within many of the relevant groups, and finding representative leadership, as well as financial support for staff and programming, is still a long way off.

Veteran ecumenists involved in the work of councils of churches are currently engaged in a vigorous debate over which direction they should seek to grow. A turn to the evangelical churches, where there is little enthusiasm for ecumenical goals, would demand considerable educational efforts, but would at least keep in focus the traditional church-uniting work of these councils. A turn to interfaith—or interreligious—partners, many of which are not structured to participate in these historic councils, would demand a considerable refocusing of statewide council efforts, but would at least keep pace with religious activity emerging in the region's cities and towns.[9]

As councils consider ways to expand their membership to include other denominations like the historically African-American churches and the Orthodox Christian churches, the number of issues and causes presented to the member churches multiplies. New ecumenical partners bring new differences as well as distinctive emphases to the circle of concerns. Protestant churches can rightfully be proud of clearing the decks of the Reformation arguments about the amount of water to use in baptism. But resolving issues that truly divide church members today, such as abortion, racism, homosexuality, and America's role in the world, need a different kind of attention and commitment from members of churches. The challenge for ecumenically minded Protestants is to find relevant and pressing issues where genuine agreement already exists so that churches can make a more immediate impact in public policy discussions.

The Episcopal bishops in New England, for instance, have recently emphasized the need for their church to speak out on threats to the environment, while Methodist pastors in the region are providing ways for their churches to be involved in anti-war protests. In surfacing these concerns, leaders can rely on the fact that New England is a more "liberal" part of the country where these political actions are more likely to resonate with the wider population, and they can also assume some degree of acceptance by church members of these campaigns since they represent convictions widely held by the national leadership of their denominations.

In early 2003, when the Rev. Mark Goad, pastor of Trinity Methodist in West Springfield, Massachusetts, began to preach about his concerns over war in Iraq and to create opportunities for his congregants to attend war protests, send rice packages to Washington, and sign petitions, he heard more than occasional grumbling over the church's involvement in political action. He characterized his congregation as a diverse group: pacifists, just-war folks, and hawks. These are not traditional Methodist theological positions, but represent the reality at the grassroots level of congregational life. Some members of Trinity have come from the South, others from the Mennonite Church (a traditional pacifist denomination), and still others are "practically Unitarian." One member, a conservative who supported the war effort, actually destroyed copies of the Methodist Bishops' statement. In serving such a constituency, Rev. Goad notes in an e-mail that the typical Methodist is pretty hard to define in these days.

Ministers are not fond of taking on members of their congregations, and know that adopting a "prophetic" stance *vis a vis* their congregants is likely to doom them to certain conflict within the congregation. The director of the Council of Churches in Bridgeport, Connecticut, reports that the days of organizing protests and of ministers taking stands in public are long gone. Rather than organize to make a statement, the more modest task of "reporting the conversation" provides a service both to ministers leading congregations and to the wider Bridgeport community. It was strangely felt by clergy that almost all of them were opposed to the war in Iraq, while almost all of them led congregations strongly in favor of the action. The council of churches provided a place for this disparity in judgment to be discussed and presented to the wider community without singling out the tensions between an individual pastor and his or her congregants. Rev. Goad in Springfield, who was willing to preach against the war, was joined by many others throughout New England. They were united in their alienation from many members of their congregations. Ecumenical leadership provided a way for ministers, at least, to have a sense of a common mind in the midst of the political discussion, even if it did not function to provide them with an organizing mechanism.

Ecumenical enthusiasm does not stir members of Protestant congregations in the ways it did during the 1960s, when couples' groups in Worcester County, Massachusetts, responding to the invitation of the progressive Roman Catholic Bishop Bernard Flanagan, hosted living room conversation sessions. Veterans of ecumenical work in central Massachusetts, such as Jennifer Johnson, still rely on the heady sense of breakthrough they experienced for the first time in an official social fellowship between Catholics and Protestants. These personal reasons for commitment are now part of the ancient past to most church members. Recent declines in membership within Protestant churches present them with more immediate needs and pressures.

The personnel and financial commitment of churches to ecumenical work correspondingly lessens as membership declines. As long as financial support for ecumenical work, as well as other denominational giving by congregations, is assessed based on membership figures that congregations report annually to their headquarters, churches are actually rewarded for reporting declines. Ecumenical councils have begun to approach individuals and other groups for additional funding to offset the declining contributions of denominations. This approach to gaining support offsets the risk of relying on the underwriting of member churches, but it risks making ecumenism the work of a few specialists rather than the central commitment of the churches.

New Dynamics in Protestant Leadership

As heady as were the days after Vatican II, when formal bilateral dialogues between Roman Catholics and Orthodox Christians and various Protestant churches commenced, and lay people for the first time felt permission to engage in joint projects with members of other churches, there are more sober sentiments now prevailing among Protestants as leaders struggle to maintain enthusiasm for supporting institutions and structures. Severe cutbacks during the first few years of the twenty-first century at the national council of the Churches of Christ and at the World Council of Churches do not bode well for the future vigor of the ecumenical movement. During the 1980s and through the 1990s, ecumenical councils in New England experienced declining support from their member denominations due in large part to the declining numbers of congregants reported by member denominations. Signs of diminished vitality among mainline Protestants are not hard to find.

Reduced support forced the Worcester, Massachusetts, Council of Churches to close in the late 1980s. The Massachusetts Council of Churches eliminated its associate director position and reorganized its staff in 1990. New England's mainline Protestants maintain their commitment, but need to generate leadership as well if they wish to continue to rely on this mechanism for extending and enhancing the public witness of their various denominations in the region.

One way in which the churches have generated some new leadership has been through the sponsorship of New England's annual summer Ecumenical Institute, an academy hosted each year by a different state and offered to any lay person interested in this form of theological education. Registrations for these programs have been modest, but by offering a regular way to orient members of churches to the history and vision of the ecumenical movement, it is hoped that a measure of enthusiasm will persist within the dedicated lay leadership of churches. Conciliar ecumenism has seen better days, but it still is the place to look for any visible, statewide, coordinated Protestant voice.

Mainline Protestant member churches were once all led by men, and one method of ecumenical leadership in the Boston area was a regular convening of the denominational heads of United Church of Christ, Methodist, Episcopal, Lutheran, Orthodox, and Roman Catholic churches. Throughout the 1980s, during a time of significant activity in the local Lutheran and Roman Catholic dialogue and the signing of several covenants by Episcopal, Lutheran, and Roman Catholic bishops, these meetings showed a very visible commitment to clergy-led forms of ecumenism. At the bimonthly meetings, church leaders were accompanied by a staff member who sat in an outer ring. There were no women present in these meetings except for the assistant director of the Massachusetts Council of Churches and the staff assistant to the Lutheran bishop, both clergywomen. The Roman Catholic Cardinal, Bernard Law, a strong presence in these meetings, was very involved at the time in promoting anti-abortion legislation. He regularly challenged the other church leaders to join him in this endeavor, all the while aware that the mainline Protestant leadership gathered around him was of an entirely different persuasion on the issue.[10]

The Roman Catholic Church became a leader in the ecumenical movement after the path-breaking Vatican II in the early 1960s. Predictably, the form of ecumenism favored by Roman Catholics was not lay oriented, but based on bilateral dialogues conducted by official, theologically trained representatives of the churches. These bilateral dialogues, which are still in process, focus primarily on research and study by church bodies who commit themselves to the search for theological agreement on areas where there has been a history of dispute. The Lutheran–Roman Catholic dialogue, as well as the Anglican–Roman Catholic dialogue, have been joined by other dialogues between churches, such as the Methodist–Lutheran dialogue and the Roman Catholic–Pentecostal dialogue. Since these official dialogues are for the most part conducted on the national or international level between two church bodies, common action or a response to contemporary problems is not a primary goal. Proponents hope that resolving theological disputes will uncover theological foundations that will help the participating churches to subsequently engage in common action.

Ecumenical dialogue has achieved notable results; Roman Catholics and Lutherans in 1998 signed a *Joint Statement on the Doctrine of Justification* and celebrated this event with joint prayer services in several New England locations, but the enthusiasm for such advances is short-lived. Decisions by these churches is perhaps of vague import to ordinary churchgoers. Even though five centuries of theological dispute over this one doctrine have been partially cleared up, and leaders say that a new stage of talks can commence, a considerable amount of theological briefing is necessary to explain the importance of the agreement to theologically trained pastors. Believers interested in action that would involve local congregations and address local issues will have to wait on the theologians for some time. In the addendum to the agreement, the particular concern of Roman Catholics that the Doctrine of Justification be interpreted in new ways for contemporary believers reflected the essential problem of theological dialogues— their subject matter and terminology is so far removed from the ordinary language of Christians that the whole enterprise of dialogue and fashioning agreement seems irrelevant.

In spite of the hurdles to generating enthusiasm, Lutheran pastors in Manchester, New Hampshire, joined the Roman Catholic Bishop, John McCormack, and his ecumenical officer in a joint press conference to mark the issuing of the statement on doctrinal agreement. The document would be meaningful for local Catholics and Lutherans, the Rev. Henry Pawluk asserted, because there were so many mixed marriages in the region. He argued that agreements that brought the churches closer together would support these couples.[11] Clearly the couples hadn't waited for their churches to inch closer together before getting married, however.

Given the advanced training now required for understanding and entering into such work, it has proved difficult for members of Protestant denominations to keep up their enthusiasm for ecumenical dialogue. Churches that also must spend resources to maintain their own institutional health cannot provide the kind of sustained leadership needed for very vigorous forms of theological encounter and commitment.

Protestant church leaders and members may well have been encouraged by the closer relations with Roman Catholics that had become possible after years of dialogue between their theologians, but they also realized that the discovery of common foundations and commitments was accompanied by the demarcation of remaining areas of disagreement.

While Protestant denominations had for some time ordained women, the Roman Catholic hierarchy made its opposition more explicit.[12] The reiteration of their traditional teaching against women's ordination on the part of the official Roman Catholic Church is of particular importance in New England now, where women have significant leadership positions in the mainline Protestant denominations. As of 2004 the Lutheran bishop is Rev. Margaret Payne; Rev. Susan Hassinger is bishop of the United Methodist Conference in New England. The Episcopal dioceses in Rhode Island, Maine, and Vermont are headed by women. Rev. Davida Crabtree is the Conference Minister of the Connecticut Conference in the United Church of Christ, and women hold many other lay and clergy leadership positions, as executive staff in denominational offices, and as teachers and leaders in congregations. Within mainline Protestant circles, these changes are eagerly received and experienced positively. In ecumenical contexts, and especially in relationship to the Roman Catholic leadership in the region, these leadership changes amplify the sense that the churches are truly moving in separate directions rather than coming closer to each other.

Collaborative Ventures

However successful these strictly ecumenical ventures prove, one of the most important continuing strengths of New England's mainline is its capacity to develop collaborative ministries and partnerships. Robert Wuthnow of Princeton University, Mark Chaves of the University of Arizona, and other scholars have demonstrated that mainline congregations are significantly more likely to maintain several connections to community and social service ventures than are Catholic or evangelical Protestant congregations.

And the spirit of mainline Protestantism still permeates New England's non-profit sector. A good example of this sort of genius for collaboration is Center City Churches, a non-profit agency sponsored by 12 downtown Hartford churches (11 of them mainline) that operates an astounding variety of educational and social-service programs in partnership with a large number of groups, ranging from the Hartford Public Schools to the United Way. Founded in 1969, Center City Churches organized Hartford's first soup kitchen for the homeless, its first shelter for AIDS victims, elaborate after-school tutorial and summer programs for disadvantaged children, the city's first group home for mental health clients, a fuel assistance program, and a number of programs for senior citizens including a weekend senior center. It provides 95,000 meals a year and marshals the activities of more than 400 regular volunteers, most of whom belong to the sponsoring churches.

Lay leaders from Episcopal, UCC, and Methodist churches in Fall River and New Bedford, Massachusetts, are also key players in a grassroots political movement called United Interfaith of Southeastern Massachusetts, which since the mid-1990s has organized a series of highly effective campaigns to galvanize government action on issues like crime, education, drug and alcohol abuse, and economic development. Its "actions" produce mass meetings of hundreds of residents who make demands on local elected officials. Similar organizations function in six other Massachusetts cities, including Brockton and Boston.

Must We Grow?

Ecumenically minded mainline Protestant congregations maintain their focus on church unity and civic involvement at some cost. When they begin to advocate for liberal causes such as gay marriage and gun control, they articulate the views that are held by a majority within their congregations but may be held less vigorously in the local culture. While mainline Protestant sentiments on these issues are not out of line with their communities, ministers and active church members are often not seen as opinion leaders of their communities. Having a progressive political stance or advocating on behalf of a worthy cause is no longer reason in itself to sway thinking in a local culture, or to draw interested people into membership. Something else is wanted from religious communities, and mainline Protestant congregations alongside their competitors are trying to figure out what that something might be.

Evangelical and conservative congregations in rural as well as suburban and metro areas keep growing. Pastors and lay leaders in mainline Protestant churches, in a belated awakening, began to study the question addressed in Dean Kelley's 1972 church-circuit best seller, *Why Conservative Churches are Growing.* Kelley argues that the strong identity fostered by conservative churches gives them an appeal that challenges more liberal mainline churches. As New England's mainline Protestants looked at their own fortunes, many have concluded that an emphasis on unity, tolerance, and civic virtue that had long inspired ecumenical Protestants was apparently not selling well, even in a region of the country long dominated by more liberal Protestant traditions. Apparently sidelined by quickly growing conservative congregations, mainline Protestants feel they can no longer rely on their traditional and historical role to grant them public prominence.

While traditional ecumenical institutions and cooperative ventures fade in visibility and appeal, more conservative forms of association may be gaining strength. A reorganized Evangelistic Association of New England, founded in 1887 as a voluntary society to promote evangelical work in the region, changed its outmoded name to become "Vision New England," a network of consultants ready to assist congregations in achieving "spiritual renewal." The traditional evangelical parlance in their brochures and promotional material celebrates the "ways that God is bringing a spiritual renewal to New England."[13]

Through the network of services provided by Vision New England, local churches can avail themselves of services and information geared toward their own growth. The association does not address itself to wider political issues, nor does it provide mechanisms for churches to speak with a common voice in the public arena. Its success could well reflect the more autonomous nature of New England's congregational style, but its focus on growth and renewal also suggests that the churches that are growing in New England belong to the more conservative, evangelical camp rather than to the traditional ecumenically minded and civically oriented Protestantism of generations ago. Perhaps a third of Vision New England's member congregations belong to mainline denominations.

Even the Lutherans, who have not been as deeply affected by declining membership, but sensed that their day of decline was also coming, began sending leaders to workshops on church growth. Vision New England runs conferences to promote contemporary worship styles and more aggressive evangelical outreach, designed to help normally staid and liturgical congregations expand along the lines of the fast growing conservative churches popping up in their communities. Ministers and musicians seek to develop techniques to foster church growth that emphasize a vibrant youth-oriented ministry, casual informality, and guitar-supported praise teams to replace the women's groups, church choirs, and hymnal-centered worship that smacks of the old days. The legacy of community involvement that defined New England's many Protestant congregations is not openly challenged with this change of focus, but the energy spent on growth and congregational health directs most resources toward parochial concerns and away from public service or wider community leadership.

The challenge facing New England's mainline Protestants today is whether these Christians will be able to continue to engage in many of the social debates that have emerged in their communities, or whether they will choose a more cautious path and devote their energies to shoring up their membership base, perhaps by mimicking techniques of the more successful yet theologically and culturally conservative evangelical movements. The social involvement of mainline Protestants through the various state and local councils of churches and in cooperation with other faith communities, may well be set aside should the churches turn in a more conservative direction in order to attract new members.

Conservatives argue that issues like casino gambling, the conflicts in the Mideast, fair trade, and globalization will be decided on the basis of political and economic considerations rather than on religious commitments, even though religious people may well have strong opinions on these issues. In the shaping of community life, however, religious commitments will be a more decisive factor in the public debate, and the historic involvement of mainline Protestants in shaping the moral, cultural, and religious dimensions of their communities is sure to be wielded in the coming debates on these issues.

On June 6 and 7, 2003, the New Hampshire diocese of the Episcopal Church USA elected the first openly gay man as its bishop. The Rev. Gene Robinson was a familiar leader in the diocese, having been an assistant to Bishop Douglas Theuner for the preceding 16 years. Supporters claimed that the election was not an attempt to make a political statement, or to 'lead' in any kind of prophetic or provocative way, even though the vote to confirm Robinson by the national assembly later that summer in August did result in the development of an organized opposition, and will most likely sever or at least diminish the strength of ties within the Anglican Communion.

North American conservatives formally joined with Anglicans from the southern hemisphere at conferences in North Carolina and Texas in early 2004 to articulate their determination to pressure the archbishop of Canterbury to commence with discipline against the ECUSA. Much of the response to the New Hampshire Diocese decision will happen in less visible but equally consequential ways. A tearful delegate at New Hampshire's assembly told National Public Radio that she would be leaving her congregation over this decision. The vote was overwhelmingly positive in the diocese, however, and was an indication that this group of the regions' mainline Protestants did not flinch in making their choice. They instead felt a kind of confidence in facing the inevitable surge of publicity that would follow.[14]

New England's Lutherans had their annual assembly during the same weekend and included a session on sexuality in their meeting. Nervous about making a decision any time soon, the Lutherans have designed a process that spends a good deal of time on teaching people in congregations how to discuss controversial issues. In a couple of years, the denomination is scheduled to make a decision on whether or not to sanction the blessing of gay and lesbian partnerships, and the ordination of openly gay and lesbian people.[15]

While the various Protestant denominations are debating this issue within their own church walls, the United Church in Jaffrey brought the issue outside and into its community. While congregations have been places that merely reflect the ongoing debates in society, the actions of the Jaffrey church, and of the Episcopal diocese of New Hampshire, in making decisions that make the news, show a reality that may be harder to see. Mainline congregations, scattered throughout New England, and self-consciously attempting to be fully engaged in their communities rather than separated, or defined in opposition to them, may now be one of the few places in communities where debates are actually conducted, and where differences of opinion are voiced and addressed.

The legacy of mainline Protestants in New England has been the role of gathering the community and of shaping its values and mores. This gathering and defining function still characterizes the self-understanding of this religious group even though diminished numbers make their voices hard to hear in their communities. Long familiar with moving into the background as other religious groups have made themselves at home in the region, mainline Protestants have persistently held onto their essential and humdrum role as guardians of community service. They have taught and modeled a Christian commitment to civility and civic engagement. One may be tempted to wish that their tribe may increase, but for now they contribute a healthy dose of modesty to the ongoing religious life in New England.

Endnotes

1. Bethany Paquin, staff reporter for the *Monadnock Ledger's* July 11, 2002 story, explained that the Jaffrey church was one of 10 among 146 congregations in the United Church of Christ's [UCC] New Hampshire conference that had adopted an Open and Affirming policy, one that states an open welcome to gay and lesbian persons to participate fully in all aspects of a congregation's work and ministry.

2. Other denominations that are known as mainline Protestant include the Presbyterian Church USA and the Disciples of Christ, but these denominations have only scattered congregations in New England.

3. Mission statement from First Congregational Church website: www.fccucc.org/aboutus/statements.asp.

4. See for example John Green, Mark Rozell and William Clyde Wilcox, *The Christian Right in American Politics: Marching to the Millennium* (Washington, D.C.: Georgetown University Press, 2003).

5. The ELCA's New England Synod compensation guidelines state that the minimum salary range for a first-time minister with between 0–5 years experience is $37,000–$42,000. In addition the congregation is responsible for health insurance, pension, housing, and other incidentals like a travel allowance. A no-frills budget for a Lutheran congregation that had modest mortgage and maintenance expenses would be about $100,000. Lutheran congregations need to have the bishop endorse each package offered its clergy. Episcopal clergy are paid by the diocese, which receives money from the congregations and dispenses it according to a schedule reflecting years of service and size of congregation. The other Protestant churches have more congregational autonomy in relationship to clergy salary, and it is generally the clergy who pay the price for this congregational freedom.

6. The cultural and economic isolation of the rural poor, and a study of their own institutional and community development in relationship to religious commitments and values, is explored by Cynthia M. Duncan in *Worlds Apart: Why Poverty Persists in Rural America* (New Haven: Yale University Press, 1999).

7. Diane Kessler and Michael Kinnamon, *Councils of Churches and the Ecumenical Vision* (Geneva: World Council of Churches, 2000): 42.

8. Minutes of New Hampshire Council of Churches board meetings, September through May, 1998-9.

9. In describing the future of the ecumenical movement in her book *Councils of Churches and the Ecumenical Vision,* Massachusetts Council of Churches director Diane Kessler makes the concluding point that "the challenge is to show that the two efforts—relating the search for Christian unity to interfaith dialogue—are complementary while resisting the notion that Christian ecumenism is somehow passé in a religiously pluralistic world" (81).

10. The author was the assistant to Bishop Harold Wimmer of the Lutheran New England Synod.

11. Henry Pawluk was quoted in the story run by Manchester's *Union Leader* on October 31, 1998, the date the statement was issued and signed at St. Ann's Church in Wittenberg, Germany.

12. The letter of instruction regarding women's roles in the church (*Mulieris Dignitatem,* "On the Dignity and Vocation of Women") was issued by Pope John Paul II on August 15, 1988. As an "apostolic letter," the instruction was not issued *ex cathedra,* in which case it would have been received as an infallible teaching, but rather on the next level down. This doesn't provide much "wiggle room" for those who have teaching or ecumenical responsibilities.

13. Vision New England material, no date, picked up August, 2002, at 468 Great Road, Acton, MA 01720.

14. National Public Radio, "Morning Edition," Sunday, June 8, 2003.

15. Lutheran terminology for gay marriage is the blessing of same-sex relationships, while the possible ordination of openly gay and lesbian persons would be restricted to those who would remain celibate, or would remain in 'committed relationships.' The ELCA study of sexuality process was commissioned by its church-wide assembly in 2001 and is scheduled to come before the church-wide assembly for a decision in 2005 (www.ELCA.org/dcs).

Chapter Four

Part II

Conservative Protestants: Prospering on the Margins

Andrew Walsh

D emographically, culturally, and politically, conservative Protestants have a weaker hold on New England than on any other region in the United States. According to the North American Religion Atlas (NARA), as of 2000 only about 27 percent of the region's Protestants and 37 percent of its Protestant congregations are evangelical. In the nation at large, the ratio of conservative to mainline Protestants is just about the reverse. But, modest as these numbers may be, they represent very substantial growth over the levels that prevailed in the mid-twentieth century, when conservative strains of Protestantism (evangelicalism, fundamentalism, and Pentecostalism), were virtually invisible in New England. The growing conservative Protestant presence in New England is significant, but the point when the balance of forces might shift still seems far off, at least partly because recent conservative growth has taken place mostly in the region's comparatively small pool of recent immigrants.

The new vitality of conservative Protestantism in New England flows from two sources: from the activities of Protestants migrating to New England and from the now-significant regeneration of pockets of conservative Protestantism that survived after the overwhelming majority of New England Protestants moved to theologically moderate and liberal "mainline" orientations in the early twentieth century. Since the late 1960s, New England's mainline—or "oldline"—Protestant denominations have been aging, losing members or growing more slowly than the population at large, while evangelical, fundamentalist, and Pentecostal groups have been growing much faster. Despite this strong and continuing trend, the mainline still enjoys a commanding lead in the region. NARA reports, for example, that there are now about 3,800 mainline Protestant congregations in the six New England states, with 1.4 million adherents. By contrast, there are about 2,204 evangelical congregations, with 381,000 adherents. New England adherents to Pentecostalism, Holiness, and Wesleyan movements add about an additional 165,000 to the conservative side. (To put everything in perspective, however, it's worth remembering that there are 5.8 million Roman Catholic adherents in the region.)

The religious history of New England has been punctuated by a number of dramatic shifts, and it's possible that another such shift may be developing as conservative Protestantism gains ground and mainline Protestantism diminishes. Nevertheless, the inundation of Catholic immigrants that took place in the middle and late nineteenth century, which shattered the homogeneous Protestant culture that prevailed in the region from the seventeenth century, is still the most important factor shaping the religious character of the region. But, to understand New England in the twentieth and twenty-first centuries, one must recall that this Catholic onslaught followed on the heels of a period of dramatic growth that had energized New England Protestantism between the 1780s and 1835. During the Second Great Awakening, revivals flourished, and nineteenth century evangelicalism took shape, along with an astonishing variety of educational and cultural institutions, and local, national, and global mission organizations. During these years, the Methodist and Baptist movements established strong footholds in New England, and the Congregational mainstream, still theologically conservative, was remarkably vigorous.

During the century-long period of cultural contestation with Catholics that followed, New England's Protestants learned to move *en bloc*. Because of the Catholic threat, in the years between 1880 and 1925 they and their institutions shifted into the theologically liberal camp, with far fewer divisions and exceptions than in other parts of the country. In particular, New England's denominational colleges and theological seminaries moved wholesale into the moderate or liberal camp. So, in the middle decades of the twentieth century, only a scattered remnant of churches and a few small educational and mission groups remained in conservative hands. Perhaps the only conservative group that retained high visibility was the Salvation Army.

Conservative Revival

Conservative Protestantism did not, however, disappear entirely. Its revival began during the 1950s, fueled by population movement, and by deliberate mission efforts launched from other parts of the nation by a large number of evangelical, fundamentalist, Pentecostal, and holiness groups.

One of the clearest signs that national religious trends are also felt in New England, if in muted ways, has been the growth of the Southern Baptist Convention since the 1950s. The Southern Baptists serve as a good illustration of the scope and limits of conservative Protestant movement into the region. The nation's largest Protestant denomination, Southern Baptists have been spreading out of their southern base since the early twentieth century. Until the end of the 1950s, there were no Southern Baptist congregations at all in New England. By 2003, 230 congregations with about 35,000 members were recorded in the Baptist Convention of New England (BCNE), the Southern Baptist umbrella organization for the region.

Indeed, by some calculations, the Southern Baptist movement grew proportionally faster in New England between 1970 and 1990 than in any other part of the country, with total growth exceeding 500 percent.[1] While Southern Baptist growth in the region has been impressive, the denomination, like other conservative Protestant groups, actually remains quite modest in size and in public impact. (In 2003, despite decades of decline, the American Baptist Churches, a relatively small, mainline Protestant denomination once called the Northern Baptist Convention, has three times as many congregations and members in New England.)

Initially, the Southern Baptist movement came to New England as a result of population movement facilitated by Uncle Sam. U.S. Air Force families transferred in 1958 to Pease Air Force in New Hampshire from Strategic Air Command bases in Louisiana and New Mexico organized New England's first Southern Baptist church. In 1960, they named their church the Screven Memorial Baptist Church, a historically conscious salute to William Screven, a Baptist pastor who, in 1683, had led a migration from South Carolina to York, Maine, to escape persecution.[2] The church gathering at Pease sparked efforts to establish more Southern Baptist churches in New England, led mostly by transplanted southerners serving at Army, Air Force, Navy, and Coast Guard bases and stations around the region. These and other early congregations were often built, in the words of one Southern Baptist gibe, "by pastors chasing southern license plates."

Eight congregations established the New England Baptist Association in 1962, with the energetic support of the Southern Baptist Convention's national Home Mission Board. By 1967, 20 congregations were in place. By 1983, there were 114 Southern Baptist churches and missions in New England with more than 13,000 members, and the movement no longer relied chiefly on members of the military and other southern transplants for its growth. That same year, the NEBC was established, which represented the evolution of New England from a Southern Baptist mission region to one with the mature structure of local churches and regional Baptist associations under a regional convention (although, in Southern Baptist strongholds, conventions are usually state-wide rather than regional entities).

During this period of surging growth, Southern Baptist churches spread out from their original clusters around major military bases and the facilities of large, national, manufacturing corporations, taking root in small towns in northern New England and in the broad arc of suburbs around Boston, as well as in suburban Connecticut. These new congregations stressed winning and nurturing souls, and their regional organizations focused almost exclusively on planting new congregations, although there was regional support for developing campus ministries and foreign missions. By 1988, the NEBC had 160 member congregations and was aiming to double in size by the mid-1990s.

Suddenly, during the 1990s, the rate of congregational growth slowed, although the total number of Southern Baptist adherents continued to rise rapidly. In addition, like the region's other conservative Protestants, the Southern Baptists experienced dramatic and unanticipated change in the composition of their membership. Those who responded most readily to Southern Baptist mission efforts were now non-English speaking immigrants and not suburban whites. The NEBC repositioned to embrace the opportunity, and by 2003 about half of its 230 member congregations were non-English speaking. The Greater Boston Baptist Association, for example, includes nine Haitian, three Brazilian, and four Latino churches, as well as churches composed of immigrants who speak Chinese, Portuguese, Greek, Korean, Arabic, Khmer, and Tagalog, among its 51 congregations.

As a result of this trend, the Southern Baptist movement now looks quite different in rural northern New England than in urbanized southern New England. In northern New England, Southern Baptist churches tend to be small, English-speaking and mostly of native heritage in membership. In Massachusetts, Connecticut, and Rhode Island, the movement is now growing fastest in poorer, older, urban centers and first-ring suburbs, and among immigrants.

During the late 1990s, the region's Southern Baptists also adjusted their mission strategy, giving more emphasis to strengthening and enlarging existing congregations, without abandoning the goal of planting new churches. "In the early decades, six out of 10 startups didn't make it," said Dr. Jim Wideman, executive director of the NEBC. "Over the last decade our survival rate for missions has been more like eight out of 10." That change has been largely attributable to improved leadership training for pastors and lay leaders, he said.

The NEBC also gets a lot of support from Southern Baptists elsewhere. It has partnerships with Baptist conventions in Virginia, North Carolina, Tennessee, Alabama, Texas, and Mississippi, which yields some funding and a considerable amount of volunteer assistance. Southern Baptist Theological Seminary in

Louisville, Kentucky, the denomination's flagship seminary, now operates a branch campus in Northborough, Massachusetts, west of Boston, that offers part-time courses of study for aspiring ministers and lay leaders.

It may make virtue out of necessity, but one of the major strengths of the Southern Baptists and other conservative Protestants groups is that they can provide part-time ministers to small congregations. The Southern Baptist Convention has never required pastors to be seminary graduates, and roughly half of the New England Baptist Convention's pastors are "bi-vocational," working lay jobs as well as pastorates. That approach, however, meets the needs of many small-town and "ethnic" congregations. In northern New England, the Southern Baptists have even placed couples in ministry, with wives working outside the home to make it possible for their husbands to do part-time pastoral work in small, rural churches.

It is fair to say that the energies of New England's Southern Baptists remain chiefly focused on evangelism and institutional stabilization. However, many individual congregations do support activities with public impact. "A lot of our churches are involved in family life and marriage issues, they support homes for unwed mothers and pregnancy centers. Many of them also do a lot of feeding and work with the homeless," Wideman said.

"At this point, we don't have a region-wide institutional strategy to affect public life," Wideman said. "We're still in somewhat of a survival mode. Twenty years from now, when we have twice as many churches, we will have the time and ability to speak out."

Hundreds of other evangelical and fundamentalist congregations are now rooted in New England. Many are, in the Baptist way, independent organizations. In addition, the Conservative Baptist Association of America currently has 132 congregations in the region. The Baptist General Conference has 62 congregations, and the General Association of Regular Baptist Churches, which split from the Northern Baptist Convention in 1932, has 18 churches.

Pentecostal churches have followed a growth trajectory quite similar to the evangelical course, with the movement beginning to grow in New England during the 1970 and 1980s. Many new congregations were established by missionaries migrating, often unsupported, into the region. One Assemblies of God missionary found his mission field by getting into his car in Pennsylvania and pointing it toward New England. He had determined, through prayer, that God would guide him to the best place to begin his work: the town where he would run out of gas. That turned out to be Southington, Connecticut, southwest of Hartford. Calvary Assemblies of God Church continues there to this day.

The Assemblies of God is now probably the largest conservative Protestant denomination in New England. It grew from 319 to 359 churches between 1992 and 2002, which also represented a slowing of the congregational growth rate during the 1980s. The number of adherents, however, grew much faster than in the 1980s, rising by 32 percent from 51,464 to 67,859. Assemblies congregations are concentrated in Connecticut and Massachusetts. In southern New England the group has a large number of Spanish-speaking and other immigrant combinations, a pattern that began to take shape as early as the 1970s. Many Pentecostal churches are also participating in a broad movement away from calling their churches names that highlight denominational identity, usually arguing that denominational labels mean little to non-churched people. For example, the First Assemblies of God Church in East Hartford, Connecticut, a large, successful, and multi-cultural congregation recently changed its name to Crossroads Community Cathedral.

Many other Pentecostal groups are now present in the region, the West Coast-based International Church of the Foursquare Gospel, for example, has 61 congregations, more than half in Massachusetts.

Churches in the holiness tradition have also been growing. The Church of the Nazarene, which has a long history in New England, now has 171 congregations and is especially strong in Massachusetts and Maine. It also operates one of the region's two Christian colleges, Eastern Nazarene College, which was founded in Saratoga, New York, in 1900 and moved to Quincy, Massachusetts, in 1919.

Regeneration

The second major stream of conservative Protestant growth stems, at least indirectly, from the tiny group of conservative Protestants that survived the great realignment of the early twentieth century. In the years after World War II, a few churches and other institutions connected with the national revival of evangelicalism and began to expand. Churches like Boston's Park Street Congregational Church, and its minister, Harold Ockenga, became important to the national movement and helped nurture local growth. A number of small, existing institutions in the region proved critical to the revival.

In the 1950s, Gordon College, a small Boston institution founded in 1889 to train missionaries, moved to a 500-acre campus on Boston's North Shore and began to grow. With support from national figures like the Rev. Billy Graham, and from Christian philanthropists, within a few decades, Gordon College had emerged as one of the nation's most prominent Christian liberal arts colleges. Along the way, it spun-off a separate, graduate-level seminary, now called Gordon-Conwell Theological Seminary, and gained strength from a merger with Barrington College, a Rhode Island institution with roots as a Bible college. Evangelical, but not denominational, Gordon and Gordon-Conwell have identified themselves mostly with the Reformed tradition and with the history of New England Protestantism. Their influence is now widespread in the region and among many conservative Protestant constituencies.

Although both institutions serve a large number of conservative Protestant groups and many independent congregations, one of the most important aims of the schools has been to encourage the revival of evangelical faith within New England's mainline Protestant denominations. And, at this point, hundreds of mainline congregations in New England—Baptist, Episcopalian, Presbyterian, United Church of Christ, and others—are now led by ministers and lay leaders who have graduated from Gordon or Gordon-Conwell.

Another revitalized organization that has gained wide influence is Vision New England, which was founded in 1887 as the Evangelistic Association of New England, a collaborative venture of seven denominations. The group now provides about 5,000 New England congregations from 80 different denominations with a variety of ministries and services. The organization itself is clearly evangelical—it subscribes to the National Evangelical Association's statement of faith—but its style and many of its programs are inclusive. At least a third of the congregations listed as members on its Web site are mainline Protestant, and a number of Roman Catholic and even one Greek Orthodox parish belong to the group. The organization's annual congress in Boston attracts more than 10,000 participants, who are largely attracted by the organization's programming, which offers practical emphasis on approaches that build stronger congregations.

Vision New England also organizes elaborate networks and training programs for clergy and lay leaders, including those working in ministries targeting men, women, children, the elderly, the deaf, the disabled, small groups, family life, and those in prisons. The organization sponsors a web of weekly prayer meetings for pastors in 75 New England towns and cities, some of which are organized by denomination (several, for example, are composed of evangelical pastors working in the liberal United Church of Christ).

The group also embodies conservative expansion along two tracks—growing openness in mainline congregations and an explosion of immigrant membership in conservative churches. "There's a hidden revival taking place in Massachusetts," Rev. David Midwood, president of the organization, said. "Right now there may be as many as 300 Brazilian congregations meeting in New England." He said he himself belongs to a largely Spanish-speaking congregation in Lawrence, Massachusetts. That old mill city now has at least 40 Spanish-speaking conservative Protestant congregations.

As Vision New England's list of supporting members makes clear, many of the region's mainline churches also have organized evangelical constituencies. "All of the mainline churches have evangelical roots and all of them have groups within them that continue to identify with evangelical faith—the Biblical Witness Fellowship in the United Church of Christ, Presbyterians for Renewal in the

Presbyterian Church in the U.S.A., the Good News Fellowship among the United Methodists," Midwood said. Indeed, some of the region's largest mainline congregations now identify with evangelicalism.

Among those most often cited as leaning evangelical is the First Church of Christ Congregational in the Hartford suburb of Wethersfield. Founded in 1634, it has long been a pillar of the United Church of Christ, one of the most liberal of the mainline Protestant denominations. First Church may well be the single largest congregation in that denomination. But, for more than 25 years, it has been firmly committed to the church-growth movement, increasingly evangelical, and moving beyond its town niche to draw from a metropolitan population interested in its evangelical identity and its special ministries, including a locally famous "divorce recovery" ministry.

Its current orientation was made clear in the fall of 2003, for example, when it sponsored a major celebration of the 300th anniversary of the birth of Jonathan Edwards with Gordon-Conwell Theological Seminary and Vision New England. The slogan on the church's Web page is "Christ-Centered, Bible-Based, Spirit-Filled," a set of specifications far more likely to appear on fundamentalist church billboards than mainline Protestant ones.

By contrast, those who log onto the Web site of Hartford's Asylum Hill Congregational Church, a revitalized 1,800-member congregation with some considerable sympathy for evangelical positions but a much stronger persisting mainline flavor, hear a voice saying "I welcome you to our historic church in the heart of the city, with a heart for the city." Asylum Hill Church probably wouldn't have scheduled Chuck Colson, the Watergate figure and evangelical guru, as a keynote inspirational, as First Church did for its Edwards conference, either.

Like most other sizeable mainline congregations, First Church, Wethersfield staffs many outreach ministries (to the town food bank, to a shelter for the homeless in Hartford, to a nursery school, to Meals on Wheels), but most of its impressive array of programs are focused on the spiritual, educational, and family needs of members. Asylum Hill Church, by contrast, does most of the same things for its congregation, but manages to spin much of its activity toward active connection with its impoverished neighborhood. As evidence of its "covenant to care," for example, Asylum Hill's Web site notes that the church donates a baby blanket to a disadvantaged newborn in honor of each child baptized in the church. It also emphasizes that it supports many social service organizations serving women and children in Hartford by making grants and annual gifts.

Another of the Hartford area's largest UCC congregations, First Church of Christ Congregational in West Hartford, also illustrates the difference in mood. On its Web page, First Church, West Hartford advertises itself as "called by God to be a center where spirituality and caring come alive in a faithful community," a church with a "commitment to encourage ministry in the West Hartford community and well beyond."

While there is no sign that First Church in Wethersfield will break its historical mainline ties, the church radiates the strong sense that evangelical groups are now its most significant partners. For example, in a statement posted on the Vision New England Web site, First Church's senior pastor, J. Jey Deifell, Jr., underscored the importance of conservative Protestant umbrella organizations like Vision New England. "I now believe that the paradigm is shifting such that ministry now takes place beyond denominational and traditional lines that once separated us. At one time, I was suspicious of para-church groups and non-reformed theologies. Now I am discovering the joy with uniting with all those whose hopes, efforts, and prayers, are witness of Jesus Christ as Lord."

So, tradition-bound, "high-steeple" mainline churches on the green can make dramatic theological changes. It is not yet clear whether New England's mainline churches that begin to move toward a strong evangelical position can or will stay in mainline organizations, or whether, over time, these new hybrids will lose the civic focus that has shaped them and the New England mainline so strongly for the past several hundred years. That is a question with considerable importance for New England.

Rarely a Megachurch to be Seen

Another distinctive feature of contemporary New England religious life is that it supports very few of the Protestant "megachurches" that are such a notable feature of the landscape in other American regions. A megachurch is usually defined as one with a weekly attendance of at least 2,000. By that standard, there are a grand total of three Protestant megachurches in the six New England states: First Cathedral, an African-American congregation in the Hartford suburb of Bloomfield, with a distinctively conservative theological and even political character; Grace Chapel, a large nondenominational evangelical congregation in Lexington, outside Boston; and the Boston Church of Christ. To put this in perspective, there are three megachurches in Mobile, Alabama.[3] And, as Stephen Prothero noted in this book's chapter on religious demography, the *average* Catholic parish in New England has 3,000 members. Many suburban Catholic parishes are far larger than that.

"I think that in New England a megachurch is a congregation with 500 members," said Wideman of the Southern Baptist convention. "The national trend at the moment is toward having either very large congregations, or very small ones. In New England, we have lots of small ones." Vision New England's Midwood takes a slightly more upbeat view, saying a solid base of sizeable evangelical or evangelically oriented congregations is now in place. "We count about 75 churches with attendance of 1,000 each week," he said. Many of these are evangelical-leaning mainline churches.

The Geography of Conservative Protestantism

But to make a significant impact on public life in a particular region, a religious group must have strength on the ground. And there are few real centers of concentration for conservative Protestantism in New England. In only one New England county, Suffolk County in Massachusetts (which includes Boston), do evangelical Protestants make up a majority of the Protestant population—56 percent according to the NARA. That figure undoubtedly reflects the Boston area's large immigrant and African-American populations. But even in Boston, the actual number of conservative Protestants is small—only about 4.6 percent of the total population. The conservative share of Protestants is also above the New England average of 27 percent in many of the counties that surround Boston: 33.3 percent in Worcester County, 32.2 percent in Plymouth County, 42 percent in Bristol County. But the evangelical share of the Protestant population is below 20 percent in much of Rhode Island, Connecticut, and western Massachusetts.

In northern New England, and especially in Maine, there are some concentrations of evangelicals. In seven of Maine's 16 counties, evangelicals make up a third or more of the total population of Protestants. Evangelicals are particularly strong in the lightly populated rural and wilderness counties of central and northern Maine, and along the New Hampshire border, although Cumberland County (metropolitan Portland) has the largest single group of evangelicals, with about 12,000, or 4.5 percent of the total population. New Hampshire has fewer noticeable concentrations of evangelicals. In most of its counties, conservatives make up between 20 and 30 percent of the Protestant population, although in Strafford County, along the Maine border, the conservative share is 33 percent, and in Hillsborough County, in the metropolitan ambit of Boston, it is almost 40 percent. Conservative Protestantism is also lightly represented in Vermont, the state with the lowest percentage of religious adherents of any sort in New England. In 10 of its 13 counties, evangelicals make up fewer than 10 percent of Protestants—ranging down to 1 percent in tiny Essex County in extreme northwestern Vermont. There is, however, a modest "evangelical belt," stretching in a vector northeastward from Burlington to the Canadian border, through Chittenden, Lamoille, and Orange counties, where the evangelical concentration ranges from 31 to 43 percent (although Lamoille County's 43 percent translates into only 1,090 souls).

Conservative Protestants as Voters

While they are not highly mobilized, conservative Protestants are the most conservative voters in New England. The 2001 American Religion Identification Survey (ARIS), a survey based on telephone interviews with a statistically valid sample of randomly selected individuals, showed that 83 percent of eligible, white evangelicals are registered to vote, a figure above the New England average of 81 percent, but well below the figures for white Catholics (89 percent) and white mainline Protestants (93 percent). In ARIS, white evangelicals are also far more likely to identify themselves as Republicans (50 percent) than are any other group surveyed. New England evangelicals are also more Republican than evangelicals in any other region of the country, except in the Pacific Northwest and in the Mountain West states (where 56 and 54 percent of white evangelicals identify as Republicans).

Surveys of actual voters, however, show a more complicated picture, one in which conservative Protestants stand out more from their evangelical peers nationwide and less from other New Englanders. Exit polls taken during presidential elections since 1992 showed that of all the nation's evangelicals, New England evangelicals are the most likely to identify as Republicans (55 percent) and also as independents (25 percent) and the least likely to identify as Democrats (17.4 percent). In most other regions of the country, the share of evangelicals who identify as Democrats is at least 30 percent.[4]

And yet, on the issues, New England evangelicals are not drastically out of step with their immediate neighbors. On abortion, 48.4 percent of New England evangelicals described themselves as pro-choice or moderate, a percentage equaled only in the Mid-Atlantic and Pacific regions. On gay rights, New England evangelicals are also clustered with evangelicals in the Mid-Atlantic and Pacific regions, with solid majorities taking liberal or moderate positions. In New England, evangelicals are also more likely than in other regions to support national health insurance and environmental protection than in other regions.

It is on economic matters that New England evangelicals stand out as conservatives. Forty-eight percent of them favor cuts in welfare spending, a far higher percentage than in any other region of the country. (In the Mountain West states 40 percent of evangelicals favor welfare cuts; in the other regions the percentage is below 38 percent.) New England evangelicals are also somewhat more enthusiastic about school vouchers (50 percent in favor, 44 percent against) than either the New England average of all voters (44 percent in favor) or the national average for evangelicals.

Given the strong recent appeal of conservative Protestantism to the region's immigrants, it is also intriguing that New England evangelicals are also far more critical of government aid to minorities than either the New England average or than their peers in the most heavily evangelical regions of the country. Forty-eight percent oppose more help for minorities, in comparison to a New England average of 35 percent. In other areas of the country, evangelical opposition to additional aid hovers in the low 40 percent range, although it does creep over the 50 percent mark in the Southern Crossroads and Pacific Northwest regions. Opposition to more aid to minorities in New England may represent a lagging indicator, since the polling data presented here merges results from a series of elections dating back to 1992. That means that in the early 1990s New England's evangelical population was far whiter and more native-stock than it is now. As New England's evangelical churches become more and more populated by minority adherents, and as more immigrants are naturalized and become voters, it will be interesting to see whether conservative voting patterns on issues like this shift.

For the Religion by Region project, John Green reanalyzed the exit polling data from recent presidential elections, taking advantage of questions that asked voters how often they attend worship services. In many regions of the country, significant differences emerged when the intensity of religious practice was made a factor in analysis. For Green's study, "high-commitment" voters were defined as those who attend worship at least once a week. "Low-commitment" voters attended less frequently. The proportion of high-commitment to low-commitment voters (and "no-commitment voters)" varies by both region and religious group. In the New England sample, high-commitment evangelical voters slightly outnumber low-commitment evangelicals on most questions, but the sample size for evangelical voters is so low (about 100 total) that the numbers must be treated cautiously.

In New England, high-commitment evangelicals are much more likely than low-commitment evangelicals to identify as Republicans (64.4 to 47.9 percent) and also much less likely to identify as independents (18 versus 35.4 percent). But in New England, low-commitment evangelicals are also less likely to describe their ideology as liberal than either the national sample of low-commitment evangelicals (23 versus 28 percent) or New England's high-commitment evangelicals, 25 percent of whom describe themselves as liberal.

But, issue by issue, New England's low-commitment evangelicals tend to cluster in the middle of the spectrum. On abortion, 37 percent of low-commitment New England evangelicals are pro-choice and 20 percent describe themselves as moderates, in contrast to their high-commitment co-religionists, only 23 percent of whom say they are pro-choice and 18 percent moderate. On environmental protection, low-commitment evangelicals were far more committed to pro-protection positions than those with high commitment, with 57 percent saying they support environmental protection, as opposed to 43 percent of high commitment evangelicals. However, on issues like school vouchers, national health insurance, and help for minorities there is only a small gap between the evangelical groups.

In fact, on many of these issues (especially environmental protection, national health insurance, and welfare spending) low-commitment evangelicals fall close to the average for New England voters of all religious groups, as well as to secular voters. Even for hot-button issues like gay rights, the situation is complex. Opposition to gay rights is also weaker among New England evangelicals than in the nation at large, with 34 percent of high-commitment evangelicals describing themselves as "anti-gay rights," in contrast to the national average of 50.6. Just over one third of low-commitment New England evangelicals are anti-gay rights.

To David Midwood, Jim Wideman, and other observers, this constellation of views suggests that the evangelical population in the region still shares the general liberal outlook of its neighbors. "The people in our churches are mostly New Englanders now, and their views pretty much reflect the attitudes of New Englanders at large," Wideman said. "As time passes, I think our people will move toward more typical Southern Baptist attitudes." In the meantime, conservative Protestant churches in the region aren't pushing any political agenda hard. Midwood said he estimates that about 30 to 40 percent of the conservative Protestant population of Massachusetts aligns itself with the Christian Right movement, a portion large enough to be significant but not to constitute a powerful voting block.

The Weak Organizational Connection to Politics

Given New England's religious demography, it is not surprising that conservative Protestants have not been a major force in New England politics. Even in the region's only politically conservative state, New Hampshire, students of religion and politics haven't found much connection between the activities of religious and political conservatives. In 2002, the political scientists John Green and Kimberly Conger did list New Hampshire as one of 18 states where the Christian Right has a moderate influence within the Republican Party, but other observers have been less persuaded.[5]

Conger and Green noted that New Hampshire's congressional delegation earned a 90 percent rating from the Christian Coalition on "key votes" during the 1990s. However, as the political scientist Michelle Anne Fistek argued in 1997, "the traditional conservatism in New Hampshire has been more individualistic—supportive of individual rights and moderate-to-liberal on social issues in contrast to the religious right." Matthew C. Moen and Kenneth Palmer have recently argued that "Republican leaders do not necessarily see religious conservatives as an asset," noting that surveys have shown declining support for religious groups in New Hampshire during the 1990s.[6]

A bit surprisingly, it is in Maine, a moderate-leaning state where abortion rights receive strong popular support, that the organized Religious Right has displayed the most muscle. During the 1980s and 1990s, conservative Protestant activists, often acting in concert with socially conservative Franco-Americans, succeeded on several occasions in mobilizing voter support, especially to oppose gay-rights initiatives. In the 1980s, a group of activist Protestants revitalized one of New England's vestigial conservative organizations, the Maine Christian Civic League (MCCL), which was founded in 1897 by Protestant temperance activists. In 1984, the MCCL demonstrated its renewed vigor by pressing a referendum campaign that overturned the Maine legislature's passage of the Equal Rights Amendment by a stunning 73 to 37 percent margin.

In 1986, the league got shellacked when voters rejected an anti-obscenity law by three to one. A decade later, teamed with other Christian Right organizations such as the Christian Coalition, the MCCL mounted a comeback. In 1995, 1997, and again in 2000, it succeeded in mobilizing rural voters to score narrow, but still surprising, victories in petition-driven referendum campaigns to overturn legislative action that had expanded legal protections for homosexuals.

So, while the Christian Right has shown more political skill and influence in Maine than in any other New England state, its scope of action seems limited. MCCL, the Christian Coalition, and other groups have shown very little clout in the legislature, and their referendum victories—with small margins—have tended to be in off-year elections in which low turnouts were an important factor. As the balance of Maine's population shifts to the urbanized and coastal counties with moderate and liberal voting records, it seems unlikely that the religious right will have more to work with.

New Allies?

Another of the most distinctive features of New England conservative Protestantism is the willingness of many conservative Protestants to work closely with Catholics, and even to say nice things about Catholicism. Conservative Protestant efforts to make a common front with Catholics on issues like abortion and gay rights have a long history, dating to the Moral Majority movement of the 1970s and 1980s. In addition, there is now a pervasive sense among politically active evangelicals that the public world is properly divided between people of faith and those without faith. "Evangelicals and serious Catholics do have a lot more in common with one another than do evangelicals and liberal Protestants," noted Vision New England's Midwood.

To get anywhere in New England public life, the support of at least a sizeable minority of the Catholic population is an absolute necessity. For the Religious Right, that was the key to victory in its recent triumphs over gay-rights legislation in Maine. And it is also clear that the leaders of institutional Catholicism, whose followers are decidedly independent-minded, are looking for new alliances with evangelicals on a variety of issues. In 2004, as the Catholic bishops mounted a large-scale campaign to block gay marriage in the wake of a Massachusetts Supreme Judicial Court decision mandating it, their chief and most effective public allies seemed to be conservative Protestant-oriented groups like the Massachusetts Family Institute.

Conclusion

Conservative Protestantism has momentum in New England. Its churches are growing. They are constructing highly visible new structures on the outskirts of many of the region's towns and cities. The movement's educational infrastructure, although small, is well organized, well-funded, and of high quality.

Conservative connections to a strong national movement are also vigorous. And yet, in comparison to its regional competitors, conservative Protestantism is still small. No one dreams of replacing the Catholic Church as the dominant faith of the region, although the long-term possibility of overtaking mainline Protestantism does suggest itself. The recent rapid growth of conservative Protestantism among the region's immigrants and minorities is impressive. But because of the small size of these populations in New England and their relative isolation from a very powerful and coherent mainstream, that victory may have only very long-term significance.

For the foreseeable future, the most valid assessment is that New England's conservative Protestants are prospering, but still dwell mostly on the margins. Over the medium term, two intriguing unanswered questions will be clarified. The first is the matter of how conservative Protestantism itself will be shaped by the large regional infusion of minority and immigrant adherents. The African-American Protestant example suggests the possibility of a theologically conservative religious community with liberal political and social views. The second matter cuts in the opposite direction. What impact will conservative Protestantism ultimately make on the internal life of the region's mainline denominations? In particular, will mainline congregations that move in a conservative direction retain their strong civic orientation? Will they act more like conservative Protestant congregations, which are typically much more inward looking? The implications for New England hyper-local culture could be significant if the mainline abandons its role as cultural custodian.

Endnotes

1. Bret E. Carroll, *The Routledge Historical Atlas of Religion in America* (New York: Routledge, 2000): 115.

2. Merwyn Borders, *The Circle Comes Full: New England Southern Baptists, 1958-1998* (Franklin, TN: Providence House Publishers, 1998): 17–18.

3. See the searchable database of megachurches maintained by Scott Thumma at the Hartford Institute for Religion Research's Web site: www.hirr.hartsem.edu.

4. Exit polling data is from the National Surveys of Religion and Politics 1992,

1996, 2000, collected at the University of Akron, John C. Green, Principal Investigator.

5. Kimberly H. Conger and John C. Green, "Spreading Out and Digging In: Christian Conservatives and State Republican Parties," *Campaigns and Elections* (February 2002): 58.

6. Mathew C. Moen and Kenneth T. Palmer, "Maine: Citizen Initiative in Northern New England," in John Green and Clyde Wilcox, eds., *Marching Toward the Millennium: The Christian Right in the States, 1980-2000* (Washington, D.C.: Georgetown University Press, 2003): 329.

CHAPTER FIVE

JEWS AND AFRICAN AMERICANS: HOLDING DOWN THE FORT

Daniel Terris

It might be said that Jews and African Americans have been animating forces for public life in New England since the first European colonists crossed the Atlantic nearly four centuries ago. Or rather, the *idea* of Jews and blacks has served as a touchstone for community-building and activism.

The Puritans famously fashioned their own worldly mission on the "type" of the Old Testament Hebrews, as they reveled in their exile, subjected themselves to scrupulous self-examination, and tried in vain to build a community life that would match their expectations and that of an exacting God. The Jewish experiment, to be sure, was superseded in the Puritan belief system by the interventions of Christ and grace, but the Old Testament provided a model of personal engagement in public affairs that had been eclipsed during much of Christian history. "New England they are like the Jews/As like as like could be," teased one seventeenth century wag. Even a century and a half later, some New England fathers of the American revolution were apt to find the roots of republicanism in the narratives of ancient Palestine.

For their part, African Americans were the stimulus for the greatest outpouring of religious civil activism in United States history. Abolitionism may or may not be credited with bringing slavery to an end, but it undeniably gave shape and coherence to a passionate sense of moral engagement with public questions. Free blacks and freed slaves, like Frederick Douglass, themselves played important parts in creating the movement, but the lasting impact was felt in the sense of triumphal possibility that followed the end of the Civil War.

Making the transition from object of public life to its subject, so to speak, has been the great challenge facing both Jews and blacks. Of course, neither group carries the symbolic freight in the twenty-first century that it bore in the seventeenth or nineteenth centuries, but each has had to accommodate itself to structures of politics and belief originally framed in its image. Jews have had to try to work their way into an Establishment culture that had long since claimed Jewish values as its own—and for which the modern variant was an inconvenience. Blacks have had to create space for their community's concerns amidst the complacency of a white community that prided itself on its historical activism and contemporary tolerance.

Tiny slivers of the population in colonial days and even through the Civil War, they remain small minorities in New England, even smaller proportionally than in other parts of the country. Black Protestants make up only 3 percent of the population of New England, less than half of their proportion (8 percent) nationwide. The dominant metropolis, Boston, remains predominantly white, despite white flight to the suburbs in the wake of the school busing controversy of the 1970s. Only in Hartford and New Haven do African Americans have the critical mass to be a dominant player in urban public life, in marked regional contrast to cities in the Mid-Atlantic, the Midwest, and the South.

Depending on how you count them, Jews make up approximately 1 or 2 percent of the New England population, about the same percentage as in the United States as a whole.[1] But in close proximity to the Mid-Atlantic's far more substantial Jewish population, New England's Jews are more acutely conscious of their numbers. Heavily concentrated in the Boston metropolitan area (250,000) and with Hartford and Fairfield County, Connecticut (each with approximately 35,000) distant seconds, the diffusion of the Jewish population into more and more distant suburbs has put increasing strain on community coherence. Add to that a fundamental concern about the very nature of Jewish identity—their own population studies point simultaneously to increased commitment and declining membership—and one understands quickly the Jewish community's preoccupation with demographics.

These two communities, however, have had a disproportionate impact on public life in New England, in large part because both communities have served as extraordinarily coherent political entities. Although their numbers in terms of the overall population are small, their presence as coherent religious populations has been more substantial. Recent data from the North American Religion Atlas (NARA) show that among religious adherents Jews emerge as the second-largest denominational group in New England, at 3 percent of the total. African-American Protestants are right behind at 2.6 percent. (They are dwarfed, of course, by the Roman Catholics, who comprise 42 percent of religious adherents, and by unaffiliated individuals, at 39 percent.) Both groups are larger than the Congregationalists, the Episcopalians, and the Methodists, the backbone groups of mainline New England Protestantism.

True, these figures might be seen as a demographic oddity, since they depend on counting the mainline denominations as separate entities, while considering diverse Jewish and African American communities in the aggregate. But the fact is that when it comes to participation in public life, both communities have tended to *act* as coherent entities, thereby magnifying their impact beyond the raw numbers.

Exit polls during the 2000 presidential election, conducted by the Bliss Center at the University of Akron, found that Jews and African Americans were far and away the most solid voting blocs among religious groups in New England for any candidate: both voted overwhelmingly for the Democratic Party. And in the important local communities where blacks and Jews are concentrated, their successes in electing candidates and setting the political agenda have been significant. There are indications in both communities, as discussed below, of cracks in their historical solidarity, but both remain significant factors in the political landscape.

Faced with their demographic challenges, both communities have consistently tried to magnify their impact on public life through alliances. African Americans and Jews have looked to the Yankee establishment for models of civic engagement—Combined Jewish Philanthropies, in Boston, followed close on the heels of the Protestant Social Gospel. They have, of necessity, sought alliances with a broadly Protestant leadership in creating favorable conditions for their own communities to thrive, and in improving the public life of the region as a whole. And, despite tensions, blacks and Jews have forged important alliances with one another in New England that have fortified both.

Blacks and Jews in New England, of course, have to contend with not just one establishment, but with two. With Catholic prominence in political life in Boston, Providence, and other New England cities, the African-American and Jewish communities have sought creative ways to influence public discourse with a slender power base.

Many differences mark the African-American and Jewish communities, but in the contemporary environment, they share a common preoccupation with the threatened disintegration of their community life. Blacks have rallied powerfully through their churches to combat the social disintegration of urban neighborhoods and have begun to try to re-create in the suburbs a critical mass to ensure a degree of community stability. Their most vibrant New England leaders have made a personal and communal crusade of rescuing black youth from the debilitating spiral of poverty, drugs, and violence. Jews have been worried about their young people for different reasons; studies show that large numbers of them may be drifting away from Judaism, leaving the future of the community in peril. The external pressures of racism and anti-Semitism persist and still command the attention of both groups; but in both cases their most passionate public engagement in recent years has been with the coherence of their communities from within.

The Jewish Story

In many ways the New England Jewish story reflects the larger American Jewish story. New England gets pride of place as the home of the New World's oldest existing synagogue, the Touro synagogue in Newport, Rhode Island, completed in 1763. By the end of the nineteenth century, strong, distinct Jewish communities had grown up in several New England cities; the twentieth century saw a steady dispersion to the suburbs, and an increasing integration of the Jewish community into the majority culture.

There were, however, distinct features to the New England Jewish landscape. The region's largest metropolis, for example, was largely untouched by the migration of Jews from post-Enlightenment Germany in the mid-nineteenth century. While cities like New York and Cincinnati became home to thousands of German Jews during the 1840s and 1850s, to the extent that pre-Civil War Jewish Boston had a national character, for example, it was principally Polish. This did not prevent intra-communal tensions between the established community and the waves of newcomers when the latter arrived in massive numbers in the 1880s and 1890s; the new arrivals from eastern Europe simply identified the resident Polish Jews as "Germans" anyway. But it did mean that, with so small an established community, power flowed swiftly to the members of the second wave of immigration, who dominated Jewish institutions by the early years of the twentieth century. Hartford, by contrast, did have a substantial early German Jewish population, and Reform Judaism took an accordingly stronger hold in Connecticut but as in Boston, the Hartford community managed to avoid schisms over difficult twentieth-century issues like Zionism.[2]

Another distinctive feature of New England Jewish history is the community's complex entanglement with institutions of higher education. While socially marginalized at Harvard and Yale, Jewish students and faculty at both campuses played a large part in developing the intellectual basis of a synthesis between Jewish culture and American life, perhaps enacted most directly by the early twentieth-century Boston intellectual, Horace Kallen, who brought the concept of "cultural pluralism" into the American vocabulary. Connections with Harvard and Yale were problematic, but the prominence of the major universities in New England public life gave the Jewish community points of access and contact with a regional elite that were not equally available in other parts of the country.

New England Jews also felt quite keenly the competitive proximity of the Catholic immigrant populations. Memoirs of mid-twentieth century New England Jewish boyhoods like those of Nat Hentoff and Theodore White are replete with stories of fear and intimidation at the hands of Irish "toughs," and the density of the Catholic population made the anti-Semitic blasts of Father Coughlin and his acolytes all the more powerful. In the post-World-War-II years,

Boston's archbishop, Cardinal Richard Cushing, made it a personal mission to begin the process of improving relations between the two communities. Nevertheless, it was not until well after Vatican II that painstaking work between Catholic and Jewish community leaders created substantial and positive interactions between the communities, in large part because Cardinal Bernard Law made these interactions one of the defining features of his leadership of the archdiocese of Boston.

The relative smallness of the New England Jewish population, combined with the relative lack of intra-communal conflict, a self-conscious marriage between Judaism and Americanism, and the persistent shadow of anti-Semitism, led to a Jewish suburban dispersal with a particular Yankee flavor. As in other parts of the country, the New England Jewish diaspora began before World War II, and took off with a vengeance in the 1950s. The trend was to move into predominantly Yankee suburbs—Brookline, Newton, and Lexington in the greater Boston area; West Hartford and Bloomfield near Hartford; Hamden, Woodbridge, and Orange in greater New Haven—and then to blend as seamlessly as possible into the suburban community life.

A striking example of this trend is the town of Sharon, Massachusetts, 20 miles southwest of Boston. A Yankee town marked by its heroine of the American Revolution, Deborah Sampson, and its longtime connections to the whaling industry, Sharon became a magnet for middle-class Jews moving from the Boston neighborhoods of Dorchester and Mattapan in the 1950s. Its Jewish population climbed quickly, but tended to downplay its distinctiveness. When the display of a Christmas tree in a local elementary school became the subject of a lawsuit that went all the way to the Supreme Court in 1962, Sharon's Jewish leaders were among the most vocal defenders of the non-religious character of the tree.

By the mid-1980s, informal surveys suggested that the population of the town was nearly two-thirds Jewish, making it nearly the only majority-Jewish community in New England. Yet the Jewish character of its communal life was muted. The Congregational and Unitarian churches dominated the town center, while the synagogues had taken root on quiet side streets. The town's public life still revolved around its historic Yankee roots.

In the metropolitan areas, the trend towards dispersal has been more marked in recent years. The areas of greatest Jewish demographic growth in the Boston area are in the western suburbs like Sudbury, Concord, and Acton—formerly Yankee enclaves that now have substantial Jewish minorities. With the major cities now virtually empty of Jews in their central urban areas, with the dispersal of Jews from the mid-sized industrial cities, and with the tendency of New England Jews to downplay their presence in suburbia, Jews have begun to worry about their ability to act in concert.

Further afield, the Jewish presence in rural New England is marked principally by its strong seasonal character. Small, year-round communities dot the New England landscape, and recent years have seen an upsurge in new congregations formed under the auspices of recent arrivals. Woodstock, Vermont, for example, is home not only to a recently formed Reform synagogue, but also to an active publisher, Jewish Lights Press. And in another Vermont community, Hasidic Jews identified with the Lubovich sect have established Eretz HaChaim, a communal experiment in evangelism that reflects the Zionist impulse to reclaim the land for the Jewish people.

Yet Jewish life is most obvious in rural New England in the summertime. Jewish families from all over the Northeast send their children to an active network of Jewish camps in all six New England states, and areas like the Berkshires in western Massachusetts are magnets for suburban Jews on holiday. The actual impact on year-round public life is minimal, but the visible Jewish summer presence creates an artificial sense of Jewish impact that counteracts the suburban tendency towards quiet assimilation.

Since the 1990s, the New England Jewish community has been simultaneously pulled in two directions. On the one hand, it has taken a lead in creating a vibrant new paradigm of tolerance and diversity in public life; on the other, it has been tempted to focus inward, out of fear that ecumenism might ultimately undermine the integrity and vitality of the Jewish community.

Jews have, of course, been active in the traditional political arena. They have been especially successful on a statewide basis in Connecticut, where its first Jewish congressman (Herbert Koppelmann) was elected in 1933, its first Jewish governor (Abe Ribicoff) in 1955, and from which Joseph Lieberman made an entry onto the national stage with his combination of liberal policy opinions, a more conservative stance on moral and social issues, and his role as the first Jew on a national party ticket when he ran for vice president with Al Gore in 2000.

Yet the bulk of Jewish engagement in local public life has come through their communal organizations. Regional federations serve as umbrella organizations for funding and shaping the agendas of a host of agencies. Under these umbrellas, an array of closely networked religious, social service, educational, cultural, and political organizations operate independently, but with considerable inter-dependence.

While synagogues are not part of a formal hierarchy, the Jewish denominations (Orthodox, Conservative, Reform, and Reconstructionist) create important alliances among congregations. Agencies like Jewish Community Centers and Jewish Family and Community Services address recreational, cultural, and social-welfare needs. Active local chapters of the American Jewish Committee, the American Jewish Congress, and local Jewish Community Relations Councils serve as points of entry into social and political issues.

The response to anti-Semitism, as embodied in one of these arms of the Jewish community, is suggestive of the ways that the New England Jewish community has looked outward and inward simultaneously. Once defensive and litigious in nature, the response to anti-Semitism was transformed in New England in the last quarter of the twentieth century into a creative opportunity for building a more inclusive public life. The leading figure in this process was Leonard Zakim, the leader of the Boston chapter of the Anti-Defamation League of B'nai B'rith (ADL).

The ADL had a long and distinguished record of rapid response to anti-Semitic words and deeds, and it retains a remarkable ability to muster community action when synagogues are defaced or swastikas appear on public structures. But under Zakim, the ADL turned its attention outward, making explicit links between anti-Semitism and other forms of racial and ethnic hostility. "A World of Difference," a flagship program in this effort, offered leadership training to teenagers from a variety of backgrounds, hosted tolerance rallies in venues as large as the Boston Garden, and developed curricula for use in schools and among youth groups. This project built on and complemented one of New England's most remarkable recent contributions to American education, "Facing History and Ourselves," an organization formed in the 1970s in Brookline, Massachusetts, by two middle-school teachers to raise young people's level of knowledge about the Holocaust.

Zakim's special talent was to frame the issue of tolerance in two directions: suggesting to the Jewish community that it benefited directly from a more inclusive environment of tolerance and understanding and also calling Jews themselves to account for their part in improving conditions for even more marginalized minorities. His magnetism and his message made him a familiar figure in the Boston scene, part of a network of influential leaders that included the religious, political, and business figures. His early death from cancer cast a pall over the local community, but the strong organization that he built at the ADL has survived him; his successor, Robert Leikind, came to Boston from the Connecticut branch of the ADL, suggesting a strong regional continuity.

Ironically, a battle over Zakim's public legacy served as an emblem both of how much progress had been made and also of its limits. In the wake of his death, a proposal surfaced to name the most prominent structure of Boston's "Big Dig," a suspension bridge over the mouth of the Charles River, in his honor. The proposal met with a groundswell of public support from among Zakim's influential downtown friends, but it met stiff resistance from residents of Charlestown, the primarily Irish-Catholic community at the other end of the bridge, best-known as the site of the battle of Bunker Hill.

As the battle heated up, sparks of prejudice flew in both directions: Jews detected anti-Semitic innuendo in the opposition to naming the bridge for Zakim, while residents of Charlestown believed that they were the victims of elitist condescension towards Boston's Catholic working class. In the end, an awkward compromise was struck: the bridge was officially named the "Leonard B. Zakim/Bunker Hill Bridge," though radio traffic reports frequently shortened this to "the Zakim."

Leonard Zakim's public and symbolic leadership had its practical and political counterpart in such organizations as the Jewish Community Relations Council and the American Jewish Committee, which made Jewish engagement in local and international political issues a priority. They have proved particularly thorny, particularly with regard to local relationships with other religious groups. The New England Jewish community has always had strong ties to Israel, and support for its government intensified in the wake of the intensified violence since September 2000. This issue has unsettled alliances between Jews and liberal Protestant groups, most notably when the leaders of the Massachusetts Episcopal Church organized public protests in recognition of Palestinian suffering in 2002.

For most of its history in the United States, the Jewish community has been preoccupied with pressures from outside: anti-Semitism first and foremost. But the release of the 1990 National Jewish Population Survey set off a tidal wave of concern across the country about the potential disintegration of the American Jewish community from within. That survey documented several alarming trends: the declining prominence of religious observance and knowledge among American Jews; the increasing diffusion of the Jewish population; and most alarming of all, an intermarriage rate that, looked at one way, suggested that more than half of American Jews were choosing partners from outside the Jewish community.

The 1990 NJPS set off a furious debate about the future of the American Jewish community, as well as considerable controversy about how precisely the data should be interpreted. The real implications of the intermarriage figures were a matter for debate; there was no doubt, however, that concern about "Jewish continuity" became the salient issue of the established Jewish community in response.

There has been a special intensity about the issue of Jewish continuity in New England. With its relatively small size, its dispersal into Yankee suburbs, and high education attainment through secular institutions, New England's Jewish community seemed more than usually vulnerable to attrition by assimilation. In addition, New England's role as a surrogate home for Jewish college students called attention to its regional role in creating an environment that would keep young Jews within the fold.

Greater Boston and other Jewish communities embarked on aggressive plans to strengthen and deepen Jewish education. This meant not only strengthening synagogue-affiliated religious schools, but also undertaking an ambitious project to increase the numbers of young people attending Jewish day schools. New schools from across the denominational spectrum came into existence in the 1990s.

Some Jewish educators were particularly concerned to develop institutions that would cross the traditional denominational boundaries. Conflicts among the Reform, Conservative, and Orthodox communities, while nowhere near as pronounced or as significant as in Israel or even in some parts of the United States, nevertheless seemed to some to be a debilitating factor for the Jewish community as a whole.

Boston's New Jewish High School (now Gann Jewish Academy), founded in the mid-1990s, was one response to this concern. When it opened, it was the only non-Orthodox Jewish high school in greater Boston, and it made a self-conscious effort to extend itself to young people across the spectrum of Jewish belief. Program development in Jewish education took aim at the adult population as well. The "Me'ah" program pioneered in Boston offered Jewish adults 100 hours of Jewish studies in a two-year evening program.

The emphasis on "Jewish continuity" has been a national concern, but its special intensity in New England owes something to the larger cultural milieu. After all, the two firmly entrenched establishments—Yankee and Catholic—have specialized in creating institutional structures designed to promote their own forms of "continuity." Even in the midst of apparent decline in the influence of Protestantism, the Yankee network of service agencies and cultural institutions has preserved a mode of community engagement. The extensive parochial education network in the Catholic community has also provided an imperfect model of community cohesion.

The Jewish community has pursued its twin agenda of intergroup relations and improved community cohesion as though they are naturally complementary. The founding and presence of Brandeis University in Waltham, Massachusetts. in 1948, represents both an extension of this trend and its limits. Brandeis was established as a Jewish-sponsored, non-sectarian institution; its first president, Abram Sachar, liked to say that Brandeis was designed to be the Jewish community's contribution to American higher education, just as the Congregationalists gave the country Harvard.

Brandeis has lived since its founding with the inevitable tension between being both an engine of cohesion for the Jewish community ("a home at last," as Sachar put it) and a beacon of tolerance and openness. (Tour guides proudly point to the way that the chapels of different faiths are designed in such a way that one never casts a shadow on another.) As the barriers to full Jewish participation at Harvard and other institutions of higher education have come down, Brandeis has struggled to define its distinctive mission. Substantial efforts in such areas as

Jewish studies and Jewish education have been developed alongside major programs to provide scholarships for minority undergraduates.

But tensions between these commitments inevitably erupt. The university has generally been reluctant to act as an institution on matters of public affairs; but in 2002, its Board of Trustees took the unusual step of withdrawing sponsorship from the local National Public Radio affiliate, objecting to what they considered NPR's anti-Israel slant in its coverage of the Middle East. The ensuing debate was a natural extension of the challenges of maintaining its dual commitment.

The African American Story

Like the Jews, African Americans in New England have focused their energies on combating the threat of community disintegration. Blacks have turned their attention to the conditions of urban neighborhoods, while at the same time beginning their own somewhat slower process of institution-building in the suburbs.

While the Jewish community has largely approached New England public life through its communal institutions, the primary vehicle for African-American engagement has been through its churches, and particularly through the work of charismatic ministers who have argued through their words and actions that public engagement is a natural extension of spiritual commitment.

The prominence of African Americans in New England religious life has been enhanced, in part, by the historical openness of the mainstream denominations. Massachusetts, for example, was the first Episcopal diocese in the country to elect an African-American bishop as its head (the Reverend John Melville Burgess), and also the first to elect an African-American woman as bishop (the Reverend Barbara Harris). Harris was the first woman elected as a bishop worldwide in the Anglican Church; she came late in life to the church after a career in business with Sun Oil. New England's Episcopal churches have also benefited in recent years from an infusion of new African-American congregants whose families come from Jamaica and other former British colonies of the West Indies. The prominence of these figures and the presence of newer congregants has brought the diversity of the black religious experience to center stage.

The widespread engagement of the black church in public life, however, has come through the work of ministers in local urban congregations. Public activism based in individual congregations is not unique to the African-American community, but it is clearly more pronounced there. The independent nature of black churches, the involvement of the laity in all aspects of congregational management, and the public profile of the ministers have all contributed to a disproportionate involvement of individual churches in addressing political and community issues.

In New Haven, for example, Peter Dobkin Hall has shown that local black churches have served as "anchors" for the revitalization of community organizations; by contrast, the African American community sponsors relatively fewer secular community-wide agencies.[3]

In recent years, New England's African-American churches have approached their community's challenges with a combination of liberal lobbying for government resources for the disadvantaged and a conservative doctrine of self-help and traditional values. Working sometimes within establishment structures and sometimes outside of them, they have dramatically changed the public face of black activism and created controversy along the way. This activism has drawn directly on the themes and methods of the Civil Rights era, but has transformed those practices into demands for reform from within as well as demands for more resources from the broader political community. Three well-known ministers, one in Boston and two in the Hartford area, are broadly emblematic of these developments.

Eugene Rivers is the pastor of a tiny congregation, the Azusa Christian Church, in Boston. In the last decade of the twentieth century and the first few years of the twenty-first, he not only seized the attention of the greater Boston area, but brought his message of street ministry and church-based activism onto a national stage. Rivers founded Azusa in 1988 after a young adulthood that included drug dealing and selling welfare checks in several East Coast cities, two years at Harvard (where he came under the influence of the political scientist Martin Kilson), work as an orderly at a psychiatric hospital, and short stints in jail.

In the early 1980s, he found himself as an apprentice at the Twelfth Baptist Church to the Reverend Michael Haynes, one of the deans of Boston's black ministry. But Rivers lost patience with what he considered the staid and settled ways of the traditional black church, so he created his own church, naming it after Azusa Street in Los Angeles, a birthplace of Pentecostalism.

Rivers quickly started attracting attention to his passionate "street ministry." Drawing on his own "outlaw" background, he struck up direct relationship with gangs in Roxbury and Dorchester, reaching out to them through a combination of street language and evangelical fervor. With other African-American ministers, he developed a "Ten Point Coalition" to reach black young people, which placed a significant onus for change on the black community at large. He mobilized his own small community to develop programs that reached youth in their own neighborhoods.

Validated by local social scientists, Rivers' work came to national prominence following the election of President George W. Bush. His dogma of self-help and Christian engagement vaulted him into the position of urban spokesman for the faith-based social-service initiatives promulgated in the early months of the administration.

Yet his mobilization of community and attention came with a modicum of controversy. Rivers has contrasted his own direct ministry sharply with the established black leadership in Boston, and he has castigated religious and secular leaders alike for their self-interest and paternalism. He has not hesitated to court media controversy; his targets included the Reverend Charles Stith, a prominent Boston minister named to an ambassadorship by President Clinton; Henry Louis Gates of Harvard (Rivers was quoted as calling him "head negro in charge" in one magazine article); and local political leaders, whom Rivers considered dishonest. He was removed from the board of the local Urban League as a result of one of these incidents. In 2003, Rivers found himself at odds with community members in his own neighborhood, after he castigated Boston's Cape Verdean community for being "leaderless in terms of male leadership."

Eugene Rivers represents one end of the spectrum of black church activism: a search for public impact and influence through the media, without taking on the burdens and necessary compromises of public office. Worried more about a cohesive grassroots community life than a cohesive leadership structure, he has forged a new, if controversial model for black church engagement.

While Rivers has worked outside the mainstream political structures, Reverend Wayne Carter has become a central figure in the Hartford political establishment. While African Americans still make up only a small fraction of the population of Boston, limiting their political influence, in Hartford their numbers are more substantial, giving the activism of the black church a significant outlet for action and influence.

Like Rivers, Wayne Carter began as the pastor of a small congregation, the Mount Moriah Baptist Church. Like the Boston minister, he actively engaged the congregation in attacking urban ills at their roots in their home community. A Hartford native, Carter is the product of an era of the increasing African-American influence following the migrations from the South and the Caribbean in the 1950s and the Civil Rights activism of the 1960s. Under his leadership, Mount Moriah grew dramatically during the 1980s and 1990s, and its pastor became a prominent member of Hartford's elite. The congregation demonstrated its commitment to taking its place alongside the major city players by investing in a new parsonage on the city's upscale Scarborough Street.

Wayne Carter eschewed Eugene Rivers' confrontational style among other black ministers in Hartford, instead bringing new life to the venerable citywide Interdenominational Ministerial Alliance, which spanned both the black and white communities of the city. The pastor's engagement in greater Hartford took a step forward in 2002, when he entered electoral politics.

For five years, Hartford's schools had been in state receivership, after an elected board had been unable to stem a marked slide in educational standards and attainment. The return of control from the state to the city called for a new board, partly elected, partly appointed. Wayne Carter entered the political fray with zest, calling his passion for education reform in Hartford a natural extension of his ministry.

Carter was not only elected to the Hartford School Board, but became its president when the new board was convened for the first time in January 2003. His election was clearly a victory for a vision of political reform growing out of the concerns of the African-American church, but this synthesis quickly became problematic once Carter held an official post. Presiding over his first meeting, Carter invoked the Lord's blessing for the work that he and other board members were undertaking, and he called upon his fellow ministers to organize an interdenominational prayer day on behalf of education later in the month.[4]

These initial gestures aroused mild concern about the place of religion in the formal public life of the city, but they marked only the beginning of the controversy. As the year progressed, the strains between Carter's church-based activism and his role as public official became more pronounced. Most dramatic were Carter's public statements on homosexuality.

Responding to developments around the country, he spearheaded public protests against gay marriage, and against the election of Eugene Robinson, an avowed homosexual, to the position of bishop in the Episcopal Church. Along with other religious leaders, Carter justified this intervention into the affairs of another church as part of his mission to stand for core values in all walks of life. His actions brought down a firestorm of criticism, with charges that he was compromising the well-being of gay and lesbian youth in the Hartford schools by participating in a moral crusade against homosexuality in his ministerial capacity.

Carter, for his part, rejected the notion that he could separate his moral commitments from his public position. Arguing that every public official brings some set of values to the table, he insisted that there was no inherent contradiction between proclaiming that homosexuality was a sin, on the one hand, and supporting programs for gay students, on the other.

"I would say to [gay students] that my personal conviction about your orientation would in no way prohibit me from doing what is right, or inhibit me from making sure you get the best education you can, and that you're protected like any other student," Carter told the *Hartford Courant*. But under pressure from critics who harped on the symbolic impact of his ministerial statements on public opinion, Carter eventually decided to skip the public protest against Bishop Robinson, even while insisting that there was no valid reason why he should stay away.[5]

Eugene Rivers and Wayne Carter represent a new type of engagement in public life for the African-American church in New England. While drawing on some of the organizational methods of grassroots activism and social service pioneered by black churches during the Civil Rights movement, the content of their message is grounded in a philosophy of self-help and traditional values that was less visible during the earlier days of public engagement. In a sense, their emergence marks the political coming-of-age of a mainstream conservative impulse in African American religious life.

The Reverend LeRoy Bailey represents another key trend: the suburbanization of the African American community. The mobility of Jewish congregations has been a well-documented phenomenon for much of the twentieth century, as synagogues followed their congregants from urban to suburban communities. In New England, the movement of the African American community has been slower, but the Hartford area is at the vanguard of what may become a more regional trend.

LeRoy Bailey became the minister of the tiny First Baptist Church of Hartford in 1971. At the time, First Baptist was a community of around 60 congregants, who had broken away from the more established Hopewell Baptist Church a few years earlier. Bailey was a dynamic figure, a young man who while a teenager had made a national name for himself as a preacher. Apprenticed to Leander Hamblin at the Golden Leaf Missionary Baptist Church in Memphis, Bailey had honed his skills in pulpits around the country, and he came to Hartford primed to lead and energize a community.

By the mid-1990s, First Baptist was thriving, building on the combination of Bailey's dynamic leadership and the growth of Hartford's African-American middle class. Now in a 1,200-seat building in the city, the church not only had a large and dedicated corps of regular attendees at worship, but it had also developed 70 "ministries" to, among others, youth, drug and alcohol dependents, and the poor.

While these ministries were clearly integral to the church's mission and spirit, Bailey's energies were focused on the growth and health of the church as an institution. Following trends established in the Midwest and the South, Bailey decided that expansion needs of First Baptist could be met only in Hartford's suburbs. Building on funds collected through the tithing of congregants, First Baptist bought a massive site on "Church Corner" in the suburb of Bloomfield, and embarked on construction of a $22 million cathedral and "life center," which opened in 1999 to great fanfare.

The new structure seats more than 3,700 people, approximately half the total congregation; the single largest church building in New England was now an African American church that its leadership dubbed "First Cathedral." Its accessories include two huge video screens and 16 monitors, as well as an eight-sided cupola topped by a 150-foot cross. The building was designed both to reflect the spiritual commitments of congregants and to make its presence known symbolically as a force in the larger community.

LeRoy Bailey has marched alongside Wayne Carter in the ministers' attempts to galvanize public opinion around moral issues. But the focus of his work is on establishing his church as a force in the institutional life of the greater

Hartford area, not only by emulating the style of the megachurches but also by developing strong relationships with white colleagues around New England and throughout the country. A more concentrated black population makes the establishment of megachurches more feasible in Hartford than in other parts of New England, but the success of First Cathedral is bound to spark emulators in areas where African Americans have made substantial inroads into the middle and upper class.

Of course, there is at the same time the danger that suburbanization could eventually minimize the impact of a coherent black community on public life. After all, the dispersal of Jews to the suburbs has compelled Jews to spend more time and energy holding their own community together, possibly at the expense of a unified impact on the larger polity. A similar trend could overtake the African-American community as well.

Certainly, as the stories of these three ministers illustrate, the unified black liberalism of the Civil Rights era can no longer be taken for granted. Some things have not changed: African Americans in New England voted overwhelmingly for Al Gore in 2000, and more than half consider themselves "liberal," a higher rate than blacks across the country, according to Bliss Center exit polling.

Yet African Americans have followed a notable New England trend in deserting the traditional party structure: 42 percent of African-American Protestants in New England are registered Independents, as opposed to just 19 percent of black Protestants, nationwide. An issue like school vouchers has likewise disrupted the familiar patterns. Building on the local self-help message of preachers like Eugene Rivers and Wayne Carter, 75 percent of African-American Protestants in New England support school vouchers. The comparable figures for the black Protestants in the Mid-Atlantic, the Midwest, and the South are 62, 52, and 43 percent, respectively. Even more remarkable, however, is the contrast with white mainline Protestants in New England, only 27 of whom support vouchers.

The rise of black Independents and the contrast between black Protestants and their liberal white counterparts on social issues could suggest that traditional alliances may be re-fashioned. The solid presence of the First Cathedral at "Church Corner" in Bloomfield is an even more tangible suggestion that the face of the religious establishment in the next century will be very different than it was in New England's first 300 years. For both the African American and Jewish communities, the creative tension between ecumenical cooperation and community cohesion both reflects the challenges faced by the traditional establishment and will, in some ways, reshape that establishment.

Endnotes

1. The ARIS data gives "Jewish by religion" as 1 percent in New England and nationally. The 2000 National Jewish Population Survey gives a figure of 5.2 million Jews nationally, closer to 2 percent.

2. Two thorough histories are available for the largest Jewish communities in New England. Jonathan D. Sarna and Ellen Smith (eds) *The Jews of Boston: Essays on the Centenary (1895-1995) of the Combined Jewish Philanthropies of Greater Boston (Boston, CSP of Greater Boston, 1995)*. David G. Dalin and Jonathan Rosenbaum, *Making a Life, Building a Community: A History of the Jews of Hartford* (New York: Holmes & Meier, 1997)

3. Peter Dobkin Hall, "Historical Perspectives on Religion, Government and Social Welfare in America," in Andrew Walsh (ed.), *Can Charitable Choice Work?* (Hartford: Leonard E. Greenberg Center for the Study of Religion in Public Life, 2001): 78-120.

4. *Hartford Courant*, January 20, 2003

5. *Hartford Courant*, August 14, 2003

CHAPTER SIX

CONCLUSION: ON COMMON GROUND

Andrew Walsh

In another time of change in New England, the nineteenth-century worthy Oliver Wendell Holmes (the famous jurist's father) gleefully compared the sudden collapse of the region's old Calvinist "Standing Order" to the disintegration of a rickety old "one hoss shay," underneath the parson driving it. It was, Holmes estimated, precisely 1855 when, after "first a shiver, and then a thrill" that New England's old order "went to pieces all at once,—All at once and nothing first,—Just as bubbles do when they are burst."

It has been a long time since the homogeneous Yankee New England was supplanted by the long contention between Yankee and Catholic. And, as the twenty-first century opens, there is no denying that new change is creeping into New England, encouraged by both immigrants from other parts of America and from the four corners of the world. What were once very sharply differentiated and competing identities rooted in religion and ethnicity have blurred to a significant degree. And yet, as the authors of this volume have tended to argue, New England's long-running and distinctive regional public culture still seems pretty sturdy, as do its religious underpinnings.

The purpose of a conclusion is to pull the strings of an argument together. This book opened by arguing that to grasp New England's distinctive regional culture one must factor in both the overwhelming demographic dominance of Catholics and the still-impressive stock of cultural capital controlled by mainline Protestant custodians. In truth, both Catholic demographic dominance and the mainline

Protestant stock of various forms of capital—especially the human capital contributed by headcounts—have diminished measurably in recent decades. This is no
longer a region where the Brahmin elite slugs it out with cardinals, Kennedys, and
a surging cohort of third-generation Irish-Americans. And yet the old order, if
muted, still functions and no serious challengers are yet in sight.

In certain ways, the most surprising thing about this is the continuing importance of the mainline Protestant contribution to New England life. It is hard to shake
370 years of history, but Yankee dominance has been slipping for a long, long time.
To understand the persistence of "Protestant" influence one must attend to several
different matters.

New England's Civil Religion Still Lives

First, Protestants still benefit enormously from their connection to the region's
institutional history and to its symbolic life. A New England variant of civil religion, complete with sacred landscapes, rites, and institutions, nourishes the region's
identity and remains closely tied to the civic style of mainline Protestantism. At the
heart of this civil religion is the institution of the town, which gives form to local
life and identity. Tiny Connecticut remains a commonwealth of 169 towns, each
jealously asserting its right to home rule, no matter how far the state succumbs into
suburban sprawl. Almost all of these towns remain demonstrably tied to a "First
Church" and usually to some sort of town green, complete with a Civil War memorial and an ancient cemetery somewhere close at hand. The forms of local government crafted by Puritans in the seventeenth century—the boards of selectmen and
annual town meetings—still endure.

These civic forms were shaped by and for Protestants, but others now inhabit
them fully. Catholics, Jews, African-American Protestants, and soon, perhaps,
Latino Protestants and Catholics, have all made comfortable adjustments to a social
and political geography mapped by town and by an ideal of very local democracy.
The rhetoric of the New England town as a school for democracy still flourishes
when speeches are given at Memorial Day celebrations. (That's Memorial Day,
with its roots in the Civil War, outranking July 4 in the New England mind.)

It is worth emphasizing that the notion of the New England town as an organ-
ic, democratic entity that bestows a common local identity on residents and tran-
scends their religious identities was developed by and for Protestants. The original
New England town was designed to be exclusive, not inclusive. The town acquired
its inclusive spin during the late nineteenth and early twentieth centuries, when the
descendents of the Puritans redefined its symbolic meaning in an attempt to persuade the Catholic hordes that the town—the public sphere—stood for democratic
values that transcend the bounds of sectarian identity, for a realm where citizens
meet together to work for the public good. When the suburbanization that followed

World War II transformed New England, it took most New Englanders not into new or drastically re-organized local jurisdictions, but rather into long-established small towns, with structures and traditions shaped by mainline Protestants.

At a second level, New England's mainline Protestants still exercise social and political leadership because they arrived first in the location where everyone else would seek to follow them: into the suburban middle class. They remain a highly mobilized group, who participate often in the political process. White New England mainline Protestants lead the nation in voter registration, with 93 percent registered, according to the 2001 American Religious Identification Survey (ARIS). Further, according to exit polling from recent presidential elections, it is mainline Protestants (and secular voters) who do most to define the region's distinctive voting patterns (with strong liberal preferences on social issues like abortion, gay rights, welfare spending, national health insurance, and environmental policy).[1]

The above notwithstanding, New England mainline Protestants are also important because they cast a lot of votes for Republican candidates. Those whose acquaintance with New England's voting patterns is limited to presidential elections (where only New Hampshire cuts against a thoroughgoing tendency to vote Democratic) may be surprised, but Republicans regularly win certain kinds of elections in New England. In 2004, five of the six New England governors were Republicans, and five of the region's 12 U.S. senators belong to the G.O.P. Outside of New Hampshire, few of these Republicans are conservatives by national standards. But New England voters often elect Republicans, especially as governors, to serve as a check on the Democratic legislatures they also tend to elect. Neither Massachusetts nor Connecticut, for example, has elected a Democratic governor since 1986. Some of the Republicans elected statewide even hark back to the old days of Yankee dominance, such as Vermont's governor Jim Douglas, a former moderator of the Vermont Conference of the United Church of Christ, and U.S. Sen. Lincoln Chafee of Rhode Island, the son of the late U.S. Sen. John Chafee, also of Rhode Island.

Surveys show that in a region where a plurality of voters are registered Democrats, mainline Protestants are still far more likely to be registered as Republicans or Independents. Exit polls taken at recent presidential elections showed that 46 percent of New England's mainline Protestants are registered as Republican and 29 percent as Independents. Only 25 percent are Democrats. Even "low-commitment" mainline Protestants (those who attend worship less than once a week) are considerably more likely than the regional average (42 percent versus 34.5 percent) to register as Republicans. Since New England's mainline Protestants are, by and large, social moderates and liberals, their insistence on registering as Republicans remains a commentary on their persistent collective identity and disinclination to identify themselves as Democrats.

Growing Out of the Catholic Ghetto

Catholic participation in New England's public life, and particularly Catholic voting behavior, remains distinctive. And because of the overwhelming size of the Catholic population and electorate, the Catholic vote goes a long way toward deciding New England elections. As James O'Toole argued in Chapter Two, in the middle of the twentieth century Catholic voting patterns were quite clear. New England Catholic voters were overwhelmingly Democratic; they were enthusiastic supports of the New Deal, especially as it benefited them; and quite often they were responsive to the leadership of the Catholic clergy and hierarchy in public matters.

In the early twenty-first century, there has been movement on many fronts. But New England Catholics, teamed with the region's African-American Protestant, Jewish, and secular voters, give the national Democratic Party one of its strongest, most reliable regional voting bases. Exit polling in presidential elections since 1992 shows that 47 percent of New England Catholics identify themselves as Democrats—a higher percentage than any other regional group of white Christians in the United States. A further 23 percent are Independents.

One of the most surprising revelations contained in this data is that in New England, "high-commitment" Catholics—those who attend Mass at least once a week— are more likely to describe themselves as both Democrats and liberals than Catholics who attend worship less frequently. Fifty-two percent of New England's "high-commitment" Catholics are Democrats—far above the national average for high-commitment Catholics of 45 percent. (In the region with the next highest percentage of high-commitment Catholic Democrats, the Mid-Atlantic, 48 percent identify themselves that way; in most other regions the percentage is below 42 percent.) To heighten the contrast, only 42 percent of New England's low-commitment Catholics call themselves Democrats. In addition, 33 percent of the region's high-commitment Catholics describe their political ideology as liberal, in contrast to the national average of 29 percent.

New England Catholics—both high- and low-commitment—are slightly more likely than their national peers to support gay rights. The two groups are not divided on a number of ideological issues—half or more of both groups support liberal positions on national health insurance, more welfare spending, and environmental protection. Both are also lukewarm in their support for school vouchers. However, the two groups of Catholics diverge on the two most divisive social issues. Low-commitment Catholics are far more likely to support gay rights (67 versus 56 percent) and abortion rights (61 versus 29 percent) than those who attend worship at least once a week. New England Catholics who attend Mass less than once a week are also far more likely to be pro-choice than low-commitment Catholics at large, 50 percent of whom are pro-choice.

In fact, the views of New England's low-commitment Catholics on these controversial issues align more closely with those of mainline Protestants and African-American Protestants than with their high-commitment co-religionists. Interestingly, the region's low-commitment Catholics are also less liberal on economic issues, and often hold a mix of views strikingly similar to the views of mainline Protestants (with 32 percent of low-commitment Catholics, 35 percent of low-commitment mainline Protestants, and 33 percent of high-commitment mainline Protestants favoring less welfare spending). Forty-three percent of low-commitment Catholics describe their ideology as conservative, compared to 43 percent of low- commitment mainline Protestants and 41 percent of high-commitment mainline Protestants. (Only 37 percent of high-commitment Catholics did so.) In most of the polls studied by the political scientist John C. Green, the sample sizes for high-commitment Catholics were slightly smaller than those for low-commitment Catholics, which seems about right for contemporary New England.

While the exit polling cited here does not provide all the information one might wish for, it seems reasonable to suggest that the high-commitment New England Catholics who are such loyal Democrats are probably older and residents of core urban areas. Low-commitment Catholics, whose opinions are liberal on issues of personal morality and more moderate to conservative on economic issues, seem to be moving toward the norms for New England's educated, middle-class, suburban Protestants. This suggests that the overlap between mainline Protestants and upwardly mobile, loosely attached Catholics is growing, and that a stable middle ground is now shared by New England's two old ethno-religious antagonists.

The exemplar of this evolution is arguably U.S. Sen. John Kerry of Massachusetts, the Democratic presidential candidate in 2004, whose Catholic identity, Brahmin social and educational credentials, and liberal politics are all familiar features of the New England scene, but are combined in ways that reflect changes since 1970. Catholic but not Irish—his paternal grandfather was a Czech Jew who converted to Catholicism, a fact that Kerry himself was not aware of until recently—Kerry represents the style and perhaps the substance of the "low-commitment" style of Catholicism that has become so important in New England. Educated at St. Paul's School and Yale, a member of the elite undergraduate club Skull and Bones, Kerry encountered few of the barriers that hindered most ambitious New England Catholics growing up before the late 1950s. His movement into the higher realms of New England political life was straightforward. After service in Vietnam and a prominent role in the anti-Vietnam War movement, he enrolled at Boston College Law School—the Catholic law school that is the royal road to Massachusetts political life. He then served as a state prosecutor, district attorney, and as lieutenant governor of Massachusetts before being elected to the U.S. Senate in 1982. Through his rise, no one connected him in any particular way with the Catholic Church or with its social teachings, nor has he ever been as engaged by public discourse about Catholicism as, say, Mario Cuomo or Eugene McCarthy. And he has never been photographed surrounded by groups of Catholic hierarchs, clergy and religious, as many of the Kennedys were. But neither did anyone in Massachusetts question his genuine commitment to Catholicism.

As is the case with many Catholics, Kerry does not say much publicly about his faith. Asked early in the 2004 campaign about his religious formation, Kerry alluded briefly to his service as an altar boy, and on Ash Wednesday he appeared on the campaign trail with a smudge of ashes on his forehead. His Catholicism is matter of fact, in the New England style. On his campaign Web site, Kerry dealt characteristically with the religion issue in the first paragraph of his biography by stating: "John Kerry was raised in the Catholic faith and continues to be an active member of the Catholic Church." That's it.

If Kerry's Catholicism is important enough to be in the first paragraph of his campaign biography, that doesn't mean that he—or the vast majority of other Catholic political figures—lines up often with the Church hierarchy on such public policy matters as abortion, same-sex marriage, or even capital punishment. To do so would be to become unelectable in "Catholic" New England. Kerry has plenty of company in the Senate—Connecticut's Christopher Dodd, Vermont's Patrick Leahy, and above all Edward Kennedy of Massachusetts are all prominent pro-choice Catholic Democrats. It is only fair to observe that almost all the region's prominent Catholic Republican elected officials—Connecticut Gov. John Rowland and the former Massachusetts governors Paul Cellucci and Jane Swift, for example—are also pro-choice.

How powerful can the Catholic Church be and how Catholic can those public officials be, if the Church's positions on matters like abortion and same-sex marriage are flouted so consistently? The answer is a bit complicated, but it goes to the heart of any explanation of the role of religion and public life in contemporary New England. The most direct response is that Catholic power in New England is limited, but quite real, and that the chief restrictions on Catholic power are enforced by the region's Catholics themselves.

A fuller response begins by noting the force of Michele Dillon's argument in Chapter Three about the internal diversity of contemporary Catholicism, in New England and in other places. "Regardless of the reasons why people chose to be Catholic," she writes, " and no matter what kind of Catholic they are—whether liberal or conservative, traditional or progressive, mystical or social activist—the most certain statement that can be offered about Catholics is that they are relatively independent and self-assured about their Catholicism."

Shaped by a regional history that has relentlessly pressed New England's Catholics to think about who is inside and who is outside the community, and why, it seems likely that most New England Catholics give priority to the voluntary

choice to be Catholic, rather than to the institutional Church's public-policy statements, which are often framed by a "natural law" perspective that asserts that
Catholic social teachings are rational and universally binding arguments, and not
the dogmatic teaching of one religious group among many. So, at least for the
moment, and especially among low-commitment Catholics, Catholic identity is
more about participation in the Catholic community, in the sacraments, and in the
life of the parish, than it is about public policy.

In addition, it seems indisputable that many of New England's Catholics have
accepted the argument about public life and religious culture that was advanced by
the region's Protestants as they attempted to divert a Catholic takeover of the
region. In this local version of America's pluralist ideology, Protestants stressed that
the demands of free and democratic community life transcended the values of any
one set of religious teaching or identities. This matter came into focus during the
very agitated Massachusetts debate over same-sex marriage. In late 2003, the state's
Supreme Judicial Court ruled that the restriction of marriage rights to heterosexual
couples violated the rights of gay and lesbian couples to equal protection under the
constitution of the Commonwealth.

For months, Massachusetts became the focal point of a national debate about
same-sex marriage and civil unions. At this writing, the Massachusetts General
Court—the state's legislature—was in the middle of a lengthy political process
intended to overturn the court's ruling by putting a constitutional amendment on a
statewide ballot. Any such vote could not take place before 2006, and in the meantime virtually all of the state's religious actors were mobilized. The patterns
revealed in this mobilization confirmed a familiar story of religion and public life
in New England.

Leading the vigorous opposition to the legalization of same-sex marriage
was Archbishop Sean O'Malley of Boston and the other Catholic bishops of
Massachusetts. In the weeks preceding special constitutional conventions in
February and March, the bishops attempted to activate their flocks to lobby the
legislature to block gay marriage. They paid for a mailing to 1 million
Massachusetts households and organized a huge network of rallies and meetings,
from parish halls to the Boston Common. They also forged alliances with a variety of like-minded religious groups—most especially conservative Protestants
and African-American Protestants, but also smaller bodies including Orthodox
Jews, Orthodox Christians, Muslims, and others. Opposing them was a smaller
but very vocal group of mainline Protestants and Reform and Conservative Jews.
Gov. Mitt Romney, a Mormon, sided with those arguing for an anti-gay marriage
amendment to the state's constitution.

Caught in the middle were the 199 members of the legislature, in their capacity as delegates to a state constitutional convention. During this period, the New

England journalistic convention of avoiding explicit discussion of the religious identities of lawmakers fell away. (Almost 70 percent of them, it turned out, were Catholics.) A two-day session of the convention that ended in deadlock in February 2004 offered an interesting barometer of religious politics in the Bay State at the dawn of the new century. According to The *Boston Globe* and *Boston Herald*, the largest single group of legislators (about 80) were aligned with the Archdiocese of Boston's position that neither same-sex marriages nor civil unions should be permitted. A group of 44 lawmakers, almost all of them Catholic, opposed same-sex marriage but wanted to send a measure legalizing civil unions to referendum. Another group of 55, including many mainline Protestants and all 13 of the Jews in the legislature, supported gay marriage.

During the debate, polls—supported by interviews in many news articles—suggested that opposition to gay marriage and/or civil unions was far stronger in the legislature than in the general Massachusetts population. U.S. Sen. John Kerry, not yet the Democratic nominee for president, staked out a position against same-sex marriage but in favor of civil unions, reflecting polling in Massachusetts that showed strong support for gay rights in most religious constituencies dating back to the early 1990s. Of 11 religious groups identified in presidential exit polls, only high- and low-commitment evangelical Protestants mustered even one-third of their New England adherents as anti-gay rights. (These polls did not ask about same-sex marriage or civil unions.) Sixty percent of high-commitment Catholics in New England favored gay rights, as did 69 percent of low-commitment Catholics.

Mainline Protestants and many Jews rushed to exploit this division between the Catholic hierarchy and laity, often using a logic familiar from earlier battles to restrict Catholic influence. "We respect the right of the Catholic Church to set its own policies and its own definition of marriage, but the Catholic Church does not have the right to impose its religious beliefs on others," Rabbi Devon A. Lerner, cochairman of the Religious Coalition for the Freedom to Marry, told the *Boston Globe* on January 17. "Equal civil marriage will not force priests, or any clergy, to change their beliefs or practices—our laws of separation of church and state guarantee that. We call upon our legislators to represent all the citizens of the Commonwealth, regardless of their religion."

During this discussion many Catholics, both inside and outside the legislature, frequently invoked Lerner's distinction between what they believed as Catholics, and what should be civil law. The *Hartford Courant*, for example, followed canvassers for "Love Makes a Family," a pro-same-sex marriage advocacy group, as they knocked on doors in suburban West Hartford. "I'm Catholic, and that's not in the belief structure, but if you're talking about civil marriage, I don't have a problem with that," Jay Corbalis told the *Courant* on Feb.15. The same day, the Lowell, Massachusetts *Sun* interviewed Rep. Kevin Murphy, "a product of Catholic schools who attends Mass faithfully." The *Sun* reported that Murphy would vote against constitutional amendments banning same-sex marriage because he understood the Supreme Judicial Court's action as a civil-rights decision. "I obviously weighed what my church felt, but I also have to understand that as a public official, I represent all of the constituents of my district. I have to do what I believe is the right thing for all my constituents."

Other Catholic legislators also applied "inside/outside" logic. The Associated Press noted that state Sen. Martin Montigny would vote for gay marriage, despite his church's teachings. "As a Catholic, I would never vote to diminish the sanctity of the church sacrament of marriage. As a human being, I will never deny someone their equal rights. It is my belief that the only requirement of civil marriage is enduring love and respect."

For many Catholic legislators and voters, it made a kind of local sense to express solidarity with Catholic understandings of sacramental marriage, while still voting to amend the constitution to permit civil unions for homosexuals, even if that left Archbishop O'Malley sputtering with frustration.

However the constitutional amendment fared, it was clear that the Catholic Church's opposition to civil unions as well as same-sex marriage was a minority position that could not prevail. And although it was less clear whether the Catholic legislators prepared to vote in opposition to church lobbying represented a growing tendency, based on trends on other social issues like birth control and abortion, the answer would appear to be yes. With survey data showing the Catholic laity looking more like non-Catholics in New England, the prospects for the Church's ability to influence public policy seem limited. Somehow, despite the overwhelming presence of Catholics throughout the region, the community-based civil religion of New England, based on the town and grounded in an aboriginal Protestantism, continues to work its will.

Endnote

1. National Surveys of Religion and Politics 1992, 1996, 2000, collected at the University of Akron by John C. Green, Principal Investigator.

APPENDIX

I n order to provide the best possible empirical basis for understanding the place of religion in each of the regions of the United States, the Religion by Region project contracted to obtain data from three sources: the North American Religion Atlas (NARA); the 2001 American Religious Identification Survey (ARIS); and the 1992, 1996, and 2000 National Surveys of Religion and Politics (NSRP).

NARA For the Project, the Polis Center of Indiana University-Purdue University at Indianapolis created an interactive Web site that made it possible to map general demographic and religious data at the national, regional, state-by-state, and county-by-county level. The demographic data were taken from the 2000 Census. The primary source for the religious data (congregations, members, and adherents) was the 2000 Religious Congregations and Membership Survey (RCMC) compiled by the Glenmary Research Center. Because a number of religious groups did not participate in the 2000 RCMS—including most historically African-American Protestant denominations—this dataset was supplemented with data from other sources *for adherents only*. The latter included projections from 1990 RCMC reports, ARIS, and several custom estimates. For a fuller methodological account, go to *http://www.religionatlas.org*.

ARIS The American Religious Identification Survey (ARIS 2001), carried out under the auspices of the Graduate Center of the City University of New York by Barry A. Kosmin, Egon Mayer, and Ariela Keysar, replicates the methodology of the National Survey of Religious Identification (NSRI 1990). As in 1990 the ARIS sample is based on a series of national random digit dialing (RDD) surveys, utilizing ICR, International Communication Research Group in Media, Pennsylvania, national telephone omnibus services. In all, 50,284 U.S. households were successfully interviewed. Within a household, an adult respondent was chosen using the "last birthday method" of random selection. One of the distinguishing features of both ARIS 2001 and NSRI 1990 is that respondents were asked to describe themselves in terms of religion with an open-ended question: "What is your religion, if any?[1]" ARIS 2001 enhanced the topics covered by adding questions concerning religious beliefs and membership as well as religious switching and religious identification of spouses/partners. The ARIS findings have a high level of statistical significance for most large religious groups and key geographical units, such as states. ARIS 2001 detailed methodology can be found in the report on the American Religious Identification Survey 2001 at *www.gc.cuny.edu/studies/aris-_index.htm*.

NSRP The National Surveys of Religion and Politics were conducted in 1992, 1996, and 2000 at the Bliss Center at the University of Akron under the direction of John C. Green, supported by grants from the Pew Charitable Trusts.

Together, these three surveys include more than 14,000 cases. Eight items were asked in all three surveys (partisanship, ideology, abortion, gay rights, help for minorities, environmental protection, welfare spending, and national health insurance). The responses on these items were pooled for all three years to produce enough cases for an analysis by region. These data must be viewed with some caution because they represent opinion over an entire decade rather than at one point in time. A more detailed account of how these data were compiled may be obtained from the Bliss Institute.

Endnote

1. In the 1990 NSRI survey, the question wording was: "What is your religion?" In the 2001 ARIS survey, the phrase, "...if any" was added to the question. A subsequent validity check based on cross-samples of 3,000 respondents carried out by ICR in 2002 found no statistical difference between the pattern of responses according to the two wordings.

BIBLIOGRAPHY

Dalin, David G. and Jonathan Rosenbaum. *Making a Life, Building a Community: A History of the Jews of Hartford*. New York: Holmes & Meier, 1997.

Demerath, N.J., III and Rhys H. Williams. *A Bridging of Faiths: Religion and Politics in a New England City*. Princeton, N.J.: Princeton University Press, 1992.

Gamm, Gerald. *Urban Exodus: Why the Jews Left Boston and the Catholics Stayed*. Cambridge, Mass.: Harvard University Press, 1999.

Hutchison, William R., ed. *Between the Times: The Travail of the Protestant Establishment in America, 1900-1960*. Cambridge: Cambridge University Press, 1990.

McRoberts, Omar Maurice. *Streets of Glory: Church and Community in a Black Urban Neighborhood*. Chicago: University of Chicago Press, 2003.

O'Connor, Thomas H. *Boston Catholics: A History of the Church and Its People*. Boston: Northeastern University Press, 1998.

Sarna, Jonathan, ed. *The Jews of Boston: Essays on the Occasion of the Centenary of (1885-1995) of the Combined Jewish Philanthropies of Greater Boston*. Boston: Combined Jewish Philanthropies of Greater Boston, 1995.

Sullivan, Robert E. and James M. O'Toole. *Catholic Boston: Studies in Religion and Community, 1870-1970*. Boston: Roman Catholic Archdiocese of Boston, 1985.

Warner, W. Lloyd and Paul S. Lunt. *The Social Life of a Modern Community*. New Haven: Yale University Press, 1941.

Contributors

Michele Dillon is associate professor of sociology at the University of New Hampshire. Her interests include religious identity and social change, the longitudinal study of the meaning and social implications of religion in individual lives, and public culture and cross-national studies of cultural conflict. Her recent publications include: *Handbook of the Sociology of Religion* (editor), published in 2003 by Cambridge University Press, and *Catholic Identity: Balancing Faith, Reason, and Power*, published in 1999 by Cambridge.

Maria Erling is associate professor of the history of Christianity in North American and global missions at the Lutheran Theological Seminary at Gettysburg. She holds a B.A. from Augustana College, an M.Div. from Yale Divinity School, and a Th.D. from Harvard Divinity School. Her research interests include congregational life and immigration to New England, and the history of religious practices. During the 1980s and 1990s, she served as a pastor, supervisor of urban missions, and ecumenical officer for the New England Synod of what is now called the Evangelical Lutheran Church in America.

James M. O'Toole is professor of history at Boston College. A specialist in American religious history and in the history of American Catholicism, he is now at work on a manuscript on the history of the Catholic laity. He holds a doctorate from Boston College and is the author of *Militant and Triumphant: William Henry O'Connell and the Catholic Church in Boston 1859–1944*, published in 1992 by the University of Notre Dame Press, as well as *Passing for White: Race, Religion, and the Healy Family, 1820-1920*, published in 2002 by the University of Massachusetts Press, and, with Daniel Quigley, is the editor of *Boston's Histories: Essays in Honor of Thomas H. O'Connor*, published in 2004 by Northeastern University Press.

Stephen Prothero is associate professor of religion, chairman of the Department of Religion, and director of the Graduate Division of Religious and Theological

Studies at Boston University. He holds a B.A. from Yale University and a Ph.D. from Harvard University. A historian of religion in America, he is a specialist in Asian religious traditions in the United States. His publications include: *The White Buddhist: the Asian Odyssey of Henry Steel Olcott,* published in 1996 by Indiana University Press; *Purified by Fire: A History of Cremation in America,* published in 2001 by the University of California Press; and *Asian Religions in America: A Documentary History,* co-edited with Thomas Tweed and published in 1998 by Oxford University Press. His most recent book is *American Jesus: How the Son of God Became a National Icon,* published in 2003 by Farrar, Straus and Giroux.

Mark Silk is associate professor of religion and public life at Trinity College, Hartford, Connecticut, and founding director of the Leonard E. Greenberg Center for the Study of Religion and Public Life at Trinity. A former newspaper reporter and member of the editorial board of the *Atlanta Journal-Constitution,* he is author of *Spiritual Politics: Religion and America Since World War II* (1998; 2nd edition forthcoming) and *Unsecular Media: Making News of Religion in America* (1995). He is editor of *Religion in the News,* a magazine published by the Greenberg Center that examines how the news media handle religious subject matter.

Daniel Terris is director of the International Center for Justice, Ethics, and Public Life at Brandeis University. He holds undergraduate and doctoral degrees from Harvard University. A former assistant provost at Brandeis, he is also the former co-director of Mosaic, an interracial community studies program at South Boston High School. He has written about twentieth century American politics, literature, and religion. He edited the volume *Catholics, Jews, and the Prism of Conscience,* published in 2002 by Brandeis, and wrote, with Barbara Harrison, *Ripple of Hope,* published in 1997 by Dutton Children's Books, and *A Twilight Struggle: The Life of John Fitzgerald Kennedy,* published in 1992 by Harper Collins.

Andrew Walsh is associate director of the Leonard E. Greenberg Center for the Study of Religion in Public Life at Trinity College in Hartford and managing editor of the Greenberg Center's *Religion in the News.* A former reporter and religion editor for the *Hartford Courant,* he holds degrees from Trinity College, Yale Divinity School, and a Ph.D from Harvard University. His scholarly work focuses on religion in American public life. He is at work on a manuscript called *Orthodox Christianity in America.*

INDEX

abolition, 123

abortion: Catholics and, 14, 51, 77–78, 99, 142, 144; conservative Protestants and, 119–20

abuse scandal, 56–58, 61–80; Catholics and, 14, 47, 51; and finances, 46, 58, 65–66, 70–72; and moral authority of Church, 52; and priests' councils, 54

activism, abuse scandal and, 64–68

Addison County, Vermont, Eastern religions in, 37–38

adherents: claimed by religious groups, 19, 20; definition of, 9; in Fairfield County, Connecticut, 93; in New England, by religious family, 30; in United States, by religious family, 31

African Americans: Catholic, 74; demographics of, 24, 124; in New England, 13, 123–25, 132–37. See also historically African American churches

African Catholics, 74

age, among Catholics, 73, 75

Al Smith Democrats, 47

American Baptists, 83, 96; congregation change among, 29, 29, 30; in New England, 109

American Jewish Committee, 128, 130

American Jewish Congress, 128

American Religious Identification Survey (ARIS), 13, 19, 26–27, 73, 116–17, 141, 149–50; limits of, 36

Amherst College, 32

Amoskeag Mills, 47–48

Anabaptists. See Pietists/Anabaptists

Andover Newton Seminary, 91–92

Angell, Kenneth, 69

Anglicans, and African Americans, 132

Annual Catholic Appeal, 66, 71

anti-Catholicism: in colonial era, 41; and mindset of Catholics, 46–47; in New England, 33, 43

Anti-Defamation League (ADL), 129

anti-Semitism, 125–26, 129

Arabic Baptists, 110

archbishops, 62–63

archdioceses, 62

Aroostook County, Maine, 27, 88

Ashland, Massachusetts, Hindus in, 37

Asian Americans: and Catholicism, 44–45; demographics of, 24; in New England, 35–36

Asian Exclusion Act, 35

Assemblies of God: congregation change among, 29, 29; in New England, 111–12. See also conservative Protestants

Asylum Hill Congregational Church, 89, 114

autonomy, Catholics and, 52

Azusa Christian Church, 133–34

FALMOUTH MEMORIAL LIBRARY

3 4105 00120731 2

DATE DUE

MAR 1 9 2005			
APR 28 2005			
FEB 2 0 2006			
AUG 1 3			

Demco, Inc. 38-293